Nurturing **Ecological** Conversion

Nurturing **Ecological** Conversion

A Group Retreat Based on the Wisdom of *Laudato Si'*

Yvonne Prowse
Trevor Scott, SJ
John McCarthy, SJ

NOVALIS

Cover design: Sandy Lampron
Cover images: Photographs – Trevor Scott, SJ, except for top left (Yvonne Prowse); church graphic: Novalis
Layout: Audrey Wells
Published by Novalis

Publishing Office

1 Eglinton Avenue East, Suite 800
Toronto, Ontario, Canada
M4P 3A1

Head Office
4475 Frontenac Street
Montréal, Québec, Canada
H2H 2S2

en.novalis.ca

Cataloguing in Publication is available from Library and Archives Canada

ISBN: 978-2-89830-199-5

Published in the United States by Loyola Press
8770 W. Bryn Mawr Avenue
Chicago, IL 60631
United States of America

loyolapress.com

USA ISBN-13: 978-0-8294-6013-1
USA ISBN-10: 0-8294-6013-6

Printed in Canada.

We acknowledge the support of the Government of Canada.

5 4 3 2 1 28 27 26 25 24

Contents

Acknowledgements

We are grateful for the generous financial aid offered by Les Jésuites du Canada/Jesuits of Canada, the Jesuit Forum for Social Faith and Justice, and the Roman Catholic Diocese of Hamilton, Ontario. Simon Appolloni, editorial director at Novalis, invited us to consider this project. Anne Louise Mahoney, managing editor at Novalis, edited and guided our text with consummate skill, wisdom, and patience. Thank you, Simon and Anne Louise, for enabling us to realize what lay *in potentia.*

Finally, we are thankful for the wisdom of Sr. Priscilla Solomon, CSJ who accompanied us in the development of an ecological retreat from which this book has emerged.

Torngat Mountains National Park, Labrador, Canada (John McCarthy, SJ)

Introduction

John McCarthy, SJ

View the David Blackwood painting *Fire down on the Labrador* (1980): https://ago.ca/events/celebrate-david-blackwood-1941-2022.

It is a haunting image. At night, under a clear, starry sky, down on the Labrador coast, a fishing schooner drifts in the cold Labrador current, ablaze. Abandoned to the frigid subarctic waters, the survivors await the dawning of day, adrift. They cling to life. Their future has yet to be assured.

Beneath this tragedy lives another world. A world deep of life, where the Leviathan swims, where most of the iceberg floats hidden. The artist reveals to us a world unknown to the fishermen shivering in the dark. A surface world replete with obvious danger and possible death. To the men in the lifeboat, tomorrow may never arrive. Survival is their immediate and obvious concern. Little thought is given to what lies way down deep. The ocean depths are dark and mysterious, a source of fear and foreboding. Yet, the image invites us to imagine other worlds way down deep. The hidden world unknown to those in the lifeboat dominates the scene. In fact, it seems more important than the surface drama.

We recognize the need for greater depth of mind and heart as we face our ecological challenges. We recognize the need to accept and embrace the full human experience of creation as we attempt to reimagine our relationship with creation. Just as Jonah was plunged into the depths of the sea after being swallowed by the whale – and sent to do the mission of God – we, too, are called to a depth of life that opens the heart to novel stirrings of conversion. Unfortunately, our vision of creation (or of nature, as most people would understand it) is often weak and shrivelled. For much of our vision, nature has been reduced to stuff "out there," known easily by simply taking a superficial look. Nature has become a background of material things with no meaning or significance beyond what our immediate senses can readily determine. The replacement of the notion of "creation" by that of the notion of "nature" is telling.[1]

The word *creation* is a theological term. It speaks of all that flows as gift or grace from a loving Trinitarian God – created by God, sustained in God, and called forth to loving eternal embrace in God. The word *nature*, on the other hand, is a scientific term, denoting that which is beyond the human, "out there," that which is to be examined, studied, understood, and eventually controlled. The term *creation* embraces all that is, including humanity (and angels), whereas the term *nature* is much more limited in scope, often denoting that which is beyond humanity and the human-created environment.

One could say that the *creation* of the first 1500 years of Christianity was eventually replaced by the *nature* of the post-Reformation, scientific age of the last 500 years or so.[2] In effect, the world of creation has ceased to exist for many people. Our imaginations have shrivelled to the much more limited world of nature. The world, once pregnant with meaning as a theophany, as a visible manifestation of the divine Trinity, now lies mute as an inert, mechanistic assortment of things. The bond between the Creator and God's creation was broken, as was the bond between humanity and the rest of creation.[3] Under the tutelage of science, nature has become a complex of natural ecosystems known only through the scientific method. Under the tutelage of economics, nature has become a storehouse of resources, the value of which is measured only in terms of the creation of financial wealth. The American theologian John Haught summed up nicely this contemporary claim that he termed scientific naturalism: "... nature is all there is and ... science is sufficient to understand it."[4]

Think of how we normally speak of nature when discussing issues of ecology and environmental protection. What type of language dominates our discourse? Does not the discourse of science, economics, technology, and politics hold sway today? When have you heard of religious, or spiritual, or sacred language in such conversations? Such language of the heart seems to bear little or no credence in the public marketplace of values. Any form of such spiritual language is relegated to the private sphere, considered as fatally subjective, too emotional, and of little use in public discourse. The result is that decisions are often made on scientific-technical terms, with the discourse often dominated by an elite of experts.

In this book, our assumption is that such a technical discourse is necessary but never fully sufficient as we face our ecological challenges. We need to apply the best of our scientific and technical knowledge. We need to manage the issue using fiscal responsibility and prudence. We must engage our political system so that creative and reasonable policies may come to bear on the issues. But these actions are secondary. They come after the fact of having decided what we value the most. Only the language of the sacred can help with that task.

This book is an invitation for you to engage that sacred language of depth, to venture deeply into our experience of creation in all its beauty and wonder. It is an invitation to engage and accept as meaningful our full human experience of nature – wonder, awe, fear, stillness, joy, care .... Most of our current public discussion of the ecological challenges does not permit such a journey. Many do not know how to even take a first step. Many are convinced that the stirrings of our interior lives have little to offer.

We are convinced, however, that if we do not pay attention to the depth discourse of spirituality, then we will never find the emotional and affective resources to forge a new, life-giving relationship with the creator Trinity, with each other, and with all creation.[5] In fact, Douglas Christie argues for the "significance of spirituality in helping us think about the meaning and significance of the natural world in our lives and formulate a meaningful response to the growing erosion of the natural world."[6] Christie focuses on the "importance of *contemplative spiritual traditions* in reshaping our ways of imaging and living in the natural world. 'Contemplative ecology' is a way of describing the effort to integrate these contemplative traditions into the larger work of ecological thought and renewal."[7]

Pope Francis understands the need for such a contemplative approach:

> If we approach nature and the environment without this openness to awe and wonder, if we no longer speak the language of fraternity and beauty in our relationship with the world, our attitude will be that of masters, consumers, ruthless exploiters, unable to set limits on their immediate needs. By contrast, if we feel intimately united with all that exists, then sobriety and care will well up spontaneously.[8]

It is in and through this contemplative stance before creation that we muster eyes that see and ears that hear the "Word" of God through God's creation.

An attentiveness to *landscape* is best achieved by an attentiveness to *inscape* – the manner in which landscapes move and engage our interior affect and intelligence.[9] Attention to the affective stirrings of our heart bears much fruit. The heart has reasons of which the mind knows little.[10]

American philosopher Erazim Kohák affirmed the same when he said that "we have lost sight of all but the most superficial outward semblance of reality, becoming ourselves Eliot's 'hollow men' amid a wasteland of hollow objects."[11] According to Kohák, this shallowness of thought results in "an ongoing, systematic depersonalization of both our conception of the world and the world of our ordinary life itself."[12] The result is often death and biocide.

In the pages that follow, we offer eight sessions of spiritual exercises meant to promote a contemplative ecology at the service of care for our common home. Six of the eight sessions focus on different landscapes: Water, Mountains, Forest, Desert, Prairie, and Human Landscapes. As bookends to these landscape sessions, we begin with a session on the wider landscapes of the cosmos and our lives and end with a session on experiencing the love of God in all things (the *contemplatio* of the Spiritual Exercises of St. Ignatius).

We decided to focus on landscapes (or biomes) rather than ecological issues, for example, for a reason. First, ecological issues come and go. We wanted something more enduring. Landscapes offered that sense of endurance. Indeed, we recognize that landscapes elicit meaning and memory, and that our nature myths have never gone away and indeed animate human culture as much as ever before.[13] Think of our notions of the "sacred mountain," the "river of life," or the "primeval forest."[14] In other words, landscapes act like David Blackwood's iceberg, considered at the beginning of this introduction. We experience but a fraction of the significance of landscapes in our daily lives. Often unknown to us lies a river of meaning that runs deep through time and culture, surfacing in varied and diverse ways throughout human history.

The exercises consist of readings, reflections, meditations, and rituals that hopefully invite the stirrings of the Holy Spirit – the giver of life – within you. Hopefully, the exercises will engage your minds and souls, your bodies and spirits, in a call to embrace a full experience of the created world. In other words, the exercises invite you to engage the creator Trinity and the boundless fecundity of the Trinity's love in creation.

Each session begins with a reflective piece on a particular landscape of the world. These opening reflections provide the co-authors' own spiritual relationship with creation. From there, we offer a series of spiritual exercises for the facilitator or participant (retreatant) in their practice of a contemplative ecology.

Weaving throughout the sessions are Scripture passages, offerings from *Laudato Si'*, poetry, thoughts from naturalists/environmentalists and literary thinkers, photographs, art, and so on from within and outside of our faith tradition.

These exercises are meant to help predispose us to the grace of God in our relationship with creation. Specifically, the exercises help us to respond to the Trinity's call to a depth of encounter, of intimacy, of ongoing relationship with creation. How, then, does this spiritual encounter open us up to care for creation? How does our care for creation call us ever more deeply into intimacy with God the Father, God the Son, God the Holy Spirit?

We invite participants to remember first-hand experiences of that landscape as well as other images they may hold. This will allow several things to emerge:

* A sharing of your experiences of nature in enlivening and imaginative ways

* An appreciation of the beauty of Earth, potentially leading you to fall ever more in love with Earth and all life
* A forum in which you may appreciate various aspects of the ecological crisis in a contemplative context
* An opportunity to bring your concern for Earth to God in prayer so that you may listen to God's response

May this book call forth your interior life of encounter with God. It is there that the world will take on its magnificence and beauty. It is in the contemplative depths of your heart and soul that you will encounter the Creator Trinity who, in turn, will find you in the heart of creation, the word and beauty of God. Let creation speak. It has a voice that longs to be heard. As Jesus invites us, "Let those with eyes see; let those with ears hear" (Matthew 13).

Blessings on your journey!

Christianity and Ecology

A Brief History

John McCarthy, SJ

A Theology of Creation

Why should Christianity concern itself with the natural world when it seems that the Christian faith concerns itself solely with the salvation of the human person or, more particularly, the salvation of the human soul?

Thus was my introduction to graduate studies in forest ecology at the University of British Columbia. The question came from a professor of forest genetics, from a sincere man steeped in trying to understand the depth of the relationship between humanity and forests across the span of human history. His question was a fair one. It expressed briefly what many Christians would assume to be the case.

What has Christianity to do with our environment, with nature, with the ecological challenges that afflict us today? Why worry about this valley of tears when we long for the heavenly banquet? Why worry about nature when it is the salvation of people that we seek? And, finally, why worry about the body when it is the salvation of the soul that is all-important?

The premise of this book is that ecology is at the heart of Christian faith.[15] Indeed, ecology is at the heart of authentic religion. The word *religion* finds its roots in *religare*, from the Latin meaning "to rebind." Authentic faith attempts to embrace in healthy tension that which has been torn asunder – body and soul, heaven and earth, science and religion, etc. Religious faith seeks the unity of all reality, and that includes all that exists in nature, all that is the foundation of our common home on earth.

It is in and through the revelation of the Trinity of Love – the Father, the Son, and the Holy Spirit – that the path of ecological conversion is best considered. The Trinity of God is revealed and understood as Creator Trinity. This very fact invites us to pause. Why is God, why is the Trinitarian God, revealed as the Creator Trinity? The Judeo-Christian scriptures are replete with the belief in a creator God.

In the Nicene Creed, we profess that we believe in God the Father, maker of heaven and earth, of all things visible and invisible; We believe in one Lord, Jesus Christ, through whom all things were made; and we believe in the Holy Spirit, the Lord, the giver of life. It took Christian thinkers several centuries to develop this formulation that we continue to profess. It is the fundamental assumption or core of our faith that gives sense to all else. It is the creator God that saves; it is the creator God whom we worship and adore.[16]

All is created – *creatio ex nihilo*.[17] Created *out of nothing* confirms the pure gratuity of all that is, all that has been, all that ever will be. This astonishing statement has yet to fully claim our imagination. How all that is came to be is another question. Our inquiring minds seek out the answers. Our scientific method has proven to be a powerful tool in that quest. With wonder as its driving force, the human work of science has opened us up to the marvels of an expanding universe, of evolving life, of the genetic basis of all life.

The doctrine of creation invites us to ponder the eternal question: Why is there something rather than nothing? We are invited to marvel at the very act of existence, the simple magnificence of being. In response, we are left with gratitude and awe as our sole response. It is from the very self of God, from the inner Trinitarian life of God, from the very heart of Love, that all exists. Thus, the radical importance of the central belief of the great Abrahamic faiths. All is created. All is gift. All is created in Love. All is created, giving glory to the truth, beauty, and goodness of God.[18] This acknowledgement invites us to live before mystery such that we can say with Pope Francis in *Laudato Si'*: "… there is a mystical meaning to be found in a leaf, in a mountain trail, in a dewdrop, in a poor person's face."[19]

Early Hebraic thought is also witness to the understanding of creation as not simply a backdrop to the human-Divine drama nor as a simple beginning to the story of salvation.[20] Creation, in and of itself, is the divine act of redemption. Creation and redemption are intimate partners in the history of salvation. The Judeo-Christian tradition came to the astounding insight of the pure divine gift of creation, in answer to the critical issue "Why is there something rather than nothing?" The answer was rooted in the eternal fecundity and grace of God.

Early Christian thought came to quickly acknowledge the risen Christ as the Cosmic Christ,[21] the first-born of all creation, in whom the fullness of creation dwelt. Christ was understood as foundational to the creation, salvation, and final fulfilment of all that exists: through Christ, all things were made; with Christ, all things were redeemed; and in Christ, all things were brought to eternal fullness in God. This Trinitarian Christology finds expression today in the Mass. At the end of the Eucharistic Prayer at Mass, the priest professes, "Through him, and with him, and in him, O God, Almighty Father, in the unity of the Holy Spirit, all glory and honour is yours, for ever and ever." Such Christocentric focus on the cosmic Christ took shape from several formative New Testament texts, including John 1:3, 10; Hebrews 1:1-2; Romans 11:36; Ephesians 1; Colossians 1:15-20; and 1 Corinthians 8:6, 15:28.

The very act of creation, the ongoing act of creation, and the "final" re-creation of "a new heaven and a new earth" (Revelation 21:1) express the salvific nature of creation. Creation, by its divine source and meaning, may be understood as the revelation of God. Creation reveals the mystery of the Trinitarian source of its foundation, existence, and hope.

Given the Church's understanding of the two books of revelation, creation and Scripture, both revelations are weaved one into the other. There exists no such thing as pure matter (or nature), in a sense, but rather a graced nature that speaks in myriad ways of the goodness and beauty of God. Creation is primarily a Word, a theophany – not mute, but pregnant with an epiphany of meaning, speaking of the Trinitarian creator. How do we live such that our senses become attuned to the Word of God speaking in and through creation?

At Christmas, we celebrate the incarnation of God in Christ Jesus, the enfleshment of God. The word *carnis* is Latin for "flesh" or "meat" – carnal desires, carnivore, chili con carne, etc. What an astonishing claim by Christianity: that the transcendent, infinite God, creator of the universe, is known to us in the flesh and blood of Jesus of Nazareth. No wonder many of Jesus' followers ceased to follow him further after he professed, "Very truly, I tell you, unless you eat the flesh of the Son of Man and drink his blood, you have no life in you" (John 6:53).

In the light of the incarnation, may we not profess that, for Christians, matter really does matter? In fact, Christianity is probably the most bodily of all religions. By assuming the flesh and blood of creatures, Jesus Christ entered the mystery of matter, indeed into the history of both cosmic and biological evolution. All matter, therefore, has ultimate meaning in the resurrection of Christ. God has accepted his creation forever. Nothing, absolutely nothing, is lost in the eternal loving embrace of God.[22]

In the Creed we profess the Holy Spirit as the Lord, the giver of life. That means all life. The Holy Spirit that gave birth to and animated the life of the early Church, where people were huddled, fearful, behind closed doors, is the same Spirit that brooded over the waters of chaos at the beginning of time, quickening chaos into creation. It is the same Spirit animating the seemingly eternal evolution of time and space. The same Spirit energizing the astounding evolutionary journey of life from times primordial. As Charles Darwin professed in the closing lines of his masterpiece on biological evolution, *The Origin of Species*,

> There is grandeur in this view of life [evolution], with its several powers, having been originally breathed by the Creator into a few forms or into one; and that, whilst this planet has gone cycling on according to the fixed law of gravity, from so simple a beginning endless forms most beautiful and most wonderful have been, and are being evolved.[23]

Charles Darwin recounts in scientific (if not also poetic) terms what Christianity may understand to be the creative workings of the Spirit, the giver of life.

The Trinity is revealed as a community of "persons." Community and relationality are at the core of the Divine. St. Damascene (675–749) coined the theological term *perichoresis*, which means "being-in-one-another."[24] The divine is not defined by one or the other person of Father, Son, or Holy Spirit but rather by the intimate relationality of one with the other – envisioned more like a free-flowing, coordinated dance among the three persons of the Trinity.

This community of divinity poses a radical question for us. If God is, "by nature," a trinity of relationships, does not this say that all creation is "by nature" relational?[25] Does not science reveal to us the same truth: that all of nature is connected, that all is related one to the other? Furthermore, may not the diversity of life on the planet be considered a manifestation of the creative fecundity of the relational Trinity that explodes into life? God is "by nature" creative, giving birth to the wonder of life around us.[26]

Laudato Si' is clear and direct to this point:

> The Father is the ultimate source of everything, the loving and self-communicating foundation of all that exists. The Son, his reflection, through whom all things were created, united himself to this earth when he was formed in the womb of Mary. The Spirit, infinite bond of love, is intimately present at the very heart of the universe, inspiring and bringing new pathways. The world was created by the three Persons acting as a single divine principle, but each one of them performed this common work in accordance with his own personal property. Consequently, "when we contemplate with wonder the universe in all its grandeur and beauty, we must praise the whole Trinity."[27]

If all created things are of God, then, by that very fact, all created things must reveal something of God. This insight was developed by St. Bonaventure, the second founder of the Franciscans, who claimed that all creation is revelatory of the inner life of God. As humans, we are made in the image and likeness of God. As well, so are all creatures, each in their own way, made to mirror something of God. And being of God, one can say that the main vocation or purpose of creation is the glory of God.[28] Is this not what we say as with one voice we proclaim the Gloria – "Glory to God in the highest ..."?

The doctrine of the Trinity offers what we may term a "mystical discourse" that invites us to engage the profound mystery of creation. The Trinitarian mystery, as the core of Christian faith, instills a sense of wonder, awe, contemplation, and praise before the word and beauty of God in creation. From this wellspring of meaning may flow our deep-rooted care of creation and the call to care for our common home.

Catholic Social Teaching and Ecology

The Church's recognition of ecology at the heart of Christian faith has developed over the past 60-plus years. Vatican Council II (1962–65), even though it did not explicitly mention the environment, set the stage for understanding humanity within the rich context of the entire created order. The Council developed a "social ecology" that put humanity in right relationship to God, to each other, and to all creation[29] – a creation that possesses a just autonomy with its own "stability, truth, and goodness."[30]

The Second Vatican Council met at the beginning of the rise of ecological consciousness. It began the same year (1962) as the publication of Rachel Carson's celebrated *Silent Spring*, which opened our eyes to the deleterious impacts of human-created chemicals in the environment.[31] Six years later, in 1968, we gazed in awe at the Earthrise photo from *Apollo* 8, the classic image of Earth from the perspective of the moon. The first Earth Day was celebrated in San Francisco on April 22, 1970. The environmental movement was born.

Responding to a growing awareness of human environmental impacts, the word "environment" made its first appearance in a papal document in 1971. In his Apostolic Letter *Octogesima Adveniens*, on the 80th anniversary of the social encyclical *Rerum Novarum*, Pope Paul VI addressed a series of social concerns, including for the first time ever in papal teaching the concern of the environment.

> Man is suddenly becoming aware that by an ill-considered exploitation of nature he risks destroying it and becoming in his turn the victim of this degradation. ...
>
> The Christian must turn to these new perceptions in order to take on responsibility, together with the rest of men, for a destiny which from now on is shared by all.[32]

Only a year later, in 1972, the United Nations Conference on the Human Environment was held in Stockholm, Sweden – the first-ever global conference on environmental issues.

It would not be until 1990 that the Holy See would promulgate the first papal message dedicated fully to ecology: Pope John Paul II's World Day of Peace message entitled *Peace with God the Creator, Peace with All of Creation*. Recognizing the ecological crisis as a moral issue, the Pope emphasized that "Christians, in particular, realize that their responsibility within creation and their duty towards nature and the Creator are an essential part of their faith."[33] This responsibility and duty are rooted in the very heart of our faith, flowing directly from our "belief in God the Creator," from our "recognition of the effects of original and personal sin," and from our "certainty of having been redeemed by Christ."[34] Twenty years later, in 2010, Pope Benedict issued his own World Day of Peace message on ecology entitled *If You Want to Cultivate Peace, Protect Creation*.

During their pontificates, both John Paul II and Benedict XVI continued to offer reflections on a theology of ecology.[35] The first-ever systematic presentation of the social teaching of the Church appeared in 2004 under the auspices of the Pontifical Council for Justice and Peace.[36] The care for ecology assumed centre stage in chapter 10 of the *Compendium*, entitled "Safeguarding the Environment." This ongoing reflection on Catholic social teaching and ecology is aided by many theologians and other thinkers who seek to rethink Christian faith and doctrine in the light of the environmental crisis.[37] As well, over these decades, many bishops' conferences worldwide offered pastoral reflections on the increasing degradation of global ecosystems and the deleterious impacts on human community.

One of the first pastoral reflections on ecology and environment, for example, was given by the Catholic bishops' conference of the Philippines. In their 1988 pastoral letter entitled *What is Happening to our Beautiful Land?* the bishops lamented the destructive and violent impacts of extensive deforestation on nature and the lives of countless people. Several years later, in 1991, the United States Conference of Catholic Bishops released their first pastoral letter on the environment: *Renewing the Earth: An Invitation to Reflection and Action on Environment in Light of Catholic Social Teaching.* The Canadian Conference of Catholic Bishops published their first pastoral letter on ecology in 2003,[38] with a second letter released in 2008.[39] Similar pastoral letters were promulgated by many episcopates around the world.

This rapid growth in systematic reflection on faith and ecology set a solid foundation for the eventual release of the first-ever papal encyclical on ecology. It would be Pope Francis, named after Francis of Assisi, the patron saint of those who promote ecology, who would present it. On May 24, 2015, *Laudato Si'* was addressed to every living person on the planet (LS #3) and was received with great anticipation worldwide. *Laudato Si'* quoted 21 episcopal documents that had already dealt with the theme of ecology, a recognition that *Laudato Si'* was built on several decades of papal and episcopal reflection, not to mention other Church writings.

Almost a decade since its release, one can say that *Laudato Si'* revolutionized the Catholic Church's perspective on care for our common home. The global response has been fruitful and positive – and it continues to animate people, particularly youth.[40]

A core focus of *Laudato Si'* is the notion of integral ecology. Pope Francis explains:

> Since everything is closely interrelated, and today's problems call for a vision capable of taking into account every aspect of the global crisis, I suggest that we now consider some elements of an *integral ecology*, one which clearly respects its human and social dimensions.[41]

For Pope Francis, *Laudato Si'* is a social encyclical, not solely an ecological or environmental one. To be sure, *Laudato Si'* is centred on care for our common home, but always in a context that includes the fullest dimension of the issues – what Pope Francis terms an *integral ecology*. As the Pope says: "We are faced not with two separate crises, one environmental and the other social, but rather with one complex crisis which is both social and environmental."[42]

The protection and wise use of the natural world is intimately linked to how we structure our economy, how we educate, how we care for our cities and towns, how we care for the poor and the voiceless – indeed, how we care for our own bodies. All is connected. All is related. Only by embracing the complex reality of the social and the ecological will we advance toward viable and positive solutions.

Facilitator and Retreatant Guide

Yvonne Prowse and Trevor Scott, SJ

This parish retreat invites us to pray with creation individually and communally – to listen to Mother Earth, even speak to her. It also invites us to listen prayerfully and attentively to our fellow participants to engage us more deeply in how God calls us to transformation and conversion.

As Pope Francis reminds us, while it is important to familiarize ourselves with the ecological language of scientists and to gain greater information, a deepening sense of integral ecology in our world is at its heart pastoral, rooted in prayerful communication with one another. This retreat is rooted in prayer as well as in meaningful, fruitful encounters with one another. This is done through a variety of individual and communal exercises. In each session, you are invited to engage with your fellow retreatants in sharing the fruits of your own prayer and your feelings about the ecological concerns and blessings introduced in these pages and arising in your heart and mind.

Group sharing is a vital, transformative part of the retreat. Sharing circles, large or small, promote prayerful listening, personal engagement, and discernment rather than debate or planning. They can be a source of support for facing challenging concerns and feelings. They can be a place for truth-telling. The exercises here are designed to allow us to speak our truth about what we see happening to Earth and how we feel about it. As Maya Angelou said, "There is no greater agony than bearing an untold story inside you."[43] In telling our truth and listening to others, we can find that many of our concerns and feelings are shared. We can also be helped when someone else widens our perspective or shares a source of hope. There are also exercises here designed to help us harvest hope and see how we are called to live in these challenging times.

Done well, the process of active engagement and sharing is not an intellectual exercise. It engages our whole being and helps us be more in touch with the movements of the Spirit within ourselves and one another. Led by the facilitator, each of us helps establish a safe environment and builds trust as we get to know one another through sharing.

This process can foster creativity and unforeseen possibilities for our growth, conversion, and transformation. But often there is a tendency to debate, preach, or seek simple solutions. Our engagement with one another in this process is not to argue or to defend our own points of view but to share honestly and to listen and receive with reverence, particularly to voices that may often have gone unheard, and to open ourselves to new ideas, hope, and transformation.

To that end, we offer the following suggestions to all participants:

* First is sage advice from St. Ignatius of Loyola when embarking on a retreat like this: We will benefit immensely by **entering into it with great spirit and generosity of heart** toward God. [SpExx 5][44] It's a choice to trust in God's wisdom and generosity and to open our hearts and minds to God.

* Each session has an **opening reflection for you to read** before coming to the session. Each reflection will take only 10 minutes or so to read, but you may need more time for a deeper reflection. If all you can do is read it quickly as you prepare to head to the gathering, then do that. But if you can, read it a day or two beforehand, and take some time to notice what it stirs in you – memories, dreams, hopes, concerns. You will get more benefit from having some time for it to percolate in you. If you wish, note on paper your reactions to the reflections.

* Likewise, each session ends with **suggestions for continuing your prayer** until the next session. These continue the themes of that session and offer ways to savour your relationship with God and creation. Some of these practices will take no extra time at all. Give yourself to them as you are able.

* **Pray as you can**, not as you can't. Some exercises and practices will resonate more in you than others. It's okay to spend more time with them. We have purposely presented a variety of approaches in the hope there is something for everyone. At the same time, something that initially does not resonate sometimes offers surprising gems. Pray to be open-hearted and open-minded and to trust the Holy Spirit working within you and within the group.

* If you hit a low place and feel discouraged or disheartened, **be gentle with yourself** and ask God for help, and perhaps name it in the group. So, too, be gentle with others. [SpExx 7]

* This is not a study course, and you are not generally helped by reading ahead to the sessions beyond the one you are in. Rather, as a retreat, it's helpful each week (or whatever your time frame is between sessions) for you to **stay with the material of that week**. This can include extras, such as an article or film that has a connection, but don't skip ahead. Savour the focus of that week, explore it further, keep praying with it. Let it work in you, even in your unconscious. [SpExx 11]

* **Do what you can**, not what you can't. You may have more or less time than others to devote to this between sessions. **Don't compare yourself to others**. And don't judge yourself.

* **Ask for grace**: Some of the prayer exercises we present suggest asking for a specific grace as you begin. This is a practice that was dear to St. Ignatius of Loyola. By asking God for that grace, we put the task of "accomplishing" it in God's hands and let go. It also gets us speaking directly to God right at the start, thus opening the communication and reminding us that we are not alone; we do this with God – or, better put, God is at work within us. It also focuses our prayer. If you find that you seem to be wandering or feel lost in your prayer, returning to the grace you are asking for can help gain your bearings.

* **Keep a journal** throughout the retreat. It can be as fancy or plain a notebook as you like. Take it with you to sessions so you can use it there as well as at home. Make notes after reflections and prayers – both at home and in the gatherings; note what happened in prayer and other exercises; note what moved you, what you're feeling, etc.

* **Commit yourself to the following six group norms**:

    - **Listen attentively**, even reverently, when others are speaking. Focus on the person speaking, not on what you will say as you await your turn. Know that you are listening to another of God's beloveds.

    - Listen **without interrupting or commenting**. It is a precious gift and makes for a safer environment that fosters deeper communication.

- Share from **your experience, your feelings, your hopes, your concerns**. It is not a time for teaching, or debating, or even "being right."

- **Share what you can**, not what you can't. If you are not ready to share when your turn comes, pass. You will have another chance at the end. Keep in mind that your sharing is an opportunity for you to name/claim your truth and have it witnessed and may be wisdom or solace for another.

- **Hold in confidence** what others share in the group. Don't relay it elsewhere. However, your own experience of the sessions is yours to share as you wish.

- If you stray outside the norms, your facilitator has the role of gently calling you back.

Guiding Points for Facilitators

Size of the group: The size of the group may vary between 8 and 18 people. Decide in advance the size of group you feel confident about facilitating. It would be advisable for larger groups to break into smaller groups for some activities.

As facilitator, you are key to **fostering an environment that is safe and respectful**, in which participants can come to trust themselves and one another. Here are some ways to help this along:

- Welcome participants.

- Prepare ahead of time and familiarize yourself with the exercises so that you are more at peace in the gathering.

- Be attentive in sharing groups. Engage in the exercises and participate in sharing when you can, rather than setting yourself apart.

- Keep the group to the allotted time.

- Help the group stay focused on the exercise at hand.

* **Establish a safe sharing/listening environment** in the first session. The first session has a segment for establishing the norms of the group. Six norms are listed on pages 20–21 above. Review these with the group and ask if they can commit to them. Note: there may be requests for some adaptations or specifications. It's best to get to a place where everyone can commit without belabouring this. At the start of the second session, you can briefly remind the group of the norms.

* If someone breaks the norms, find a way to **gently bring them back**. (This is one of the norms to which everyone agrees.) It's best to do this in the group, but without shaming. This way the group is reassured.

* View the people in the retreat with **warmth and respect**. Trust and honour their willingness to be there. Trust the wisdom in them.

* Trust the wisdom and the movement of the **Holy Spirit** in the group as well.

* As Joanna Macy so aptly points out, "From this trust flows **your naturalness and spontaneity**," which is essential.[45]

* Be as comfortable as you can, and **stay grounded**, especially when strong emotions are expressed in the group. And hopefully they will be at times. Fear, anger, and grief are part of facing the ecological crises and devastation of our time. Expressing them in the group can help shift them and allow God to do amazing things in individuals and in the group.

* You might keep in mind and heart St. Paul's prayer: "Glory to you, O **God, whose power at work within each of us** can do infinitely more than we can ask or even imagine." [Ephesians 3:20-21]

For exercises that involve sharing:

* **Size of sharing circle:** To give a satisfying time for everyone in a sharing circle to speak through rounds of sharing, try to limit circles to around 6 or 7 people, including the facilitator. If everyone is given around 3 minutes to share, this would calculate to around 20 minutes for each round of sharing for the entire circle per question or reflection.

* **Clarify the speaking order**: It eases people's minds to know the order in which sharing will happen. In the group sharing exercises in this book, we suggest sitting in a circle (or a few smaller circles). In this case, the order is to go around the group. You designate where it begins. That can be with whomever wishes to start. Specify also which direction (to the right or left).

  In virtual gatherings, you can list the speaking order in the chat box for everyone to see.

* **Give participants a silent minute or two for reflection *before* beginning each round** of sharing so they can focus on the new question being shared on and can enter a new space of listening to others on the new reflection question.

* **Encourage everyone to share** in your small group. But it is not necessary that everyone share. If someone prefers to pass, come back to them at the conclusion of the circle to see if they would like to share then.

* **Keep time in the group.** An overall time for group sharing is given with each exercise. Figure out how much time that takes per person. Establish a gentle way of letting a speaker know if they are going overtime and communicate that to the group. A gentle chime (not a harsh bell) is one option that is usually well received.

* **Help to maintain group focus on each question.** Some people in your circle may unintentionally share on something completely unrelated to the question being focused upon by the group. If you feel this has been happening and is disrupting or blocking the group, try not to cut that person off, but afterward do gently remind the group of the focus.

* **Reflection questions are meant to stimulate sharing and dialogue.** There is no need to feel that all the suggested questions from the activity must be shared upon. Feel free to alter the questions as well, based on your group's discussion.

* **Possible second round:** Time permitting, you can choose to have a second round of sharing if this helps draw out more or deepen the sharing. "What have you heard?" or "What commonalities do you hear?" can be helpful focus questions for a possible second round of sharing.

Adapting this resource for your situation

This program is designed primarily as a weekly program, completing one session per week. However, it can be adapted to your group's needs and availability: e.g., meet twice monthly; gather for two days for four to six sessions of your choosing; etc. Sessions can also be held online, though each participant will need to gather the required materials.

Session 1

What Landscapes Formed Me?

Opening Reflection

Yvonne Prowse

Landscape is the firstborn of creation.
Landscape has a soul and a presence,
and landscape
—living in the mode of silence—is always wrapped in seamless prayer.

—John O'Donohue[46]

What landscape(s) formed you? We three authors had a friend/fellow Jesuit from Prince Edward Island. He could wax eloquently about summers running barefoot on his aunt's farm, playing on the ocean beaches, tilling the red earth, and many aspects of his everyday island life that had a deep and formative impact on him. For another friend, it is the spaciousness of the prairies that rooted her life. For yet another, the culture and bustle growing up in a caring family in urban Montreal gave sense to their life.

It is not just a question of where you grew up or have lived. Rather, what landscapes shaped your beliefs, your dreams, your view of yourself, of God, of life, your values, personality, interactions?

Oddly enough, I was in part shaped by a landscape I have never had the opportunity to live in. Growing up in a somewhat densely packed suburb in the vast sea of suburbs of New York City, I longed for open space – specifically the big vistas, clear skies, and open hills of Wyoming – and a horse on which to explore it all, not following a grid of suburban streets and maze of highways. Where did the image of Wyoming even come from to infuse my seven-year-old heart and mind? A nature show on TV is all I can think of.

Despite our proximity to New York City, we could still see a good deal of stars in the night sky when I was a child. That is another of my formative landscapes… or skyscapes. Dad would take us out with star charts, point out various constellations, tell us how people used to navigate by the stars, how our orientation to them changes with the seasons, how it is a whole different map in the southern hemisphere. It was special to be in the quiet of the night, exploring the vast heavens. And it gave me the legacy of feeling connected to the holy whenever gazing at the night sky.

Then there is the tiny landscape of our yard and street. The apple tree that served as home base in games of tag. The cherry tree that the birds always feasted on before we could get to the fruit. The great fun of extended-family picnics. We learned freedom, play, and love in that yard. I discovered the treasure of gardening there. The simple lifestyle I have lived out for many years also began there.

Rocky Mountains, Alberta, Canada (Yvonne Prowse)

Then there was the quiet of a snowy morning as a blizzard was ending, before the plows had been through, drifts taller than the basement door, when I was the first out of the house and seemingly the only person up in the vicinity. Such a hush… filled with Presence. This is one of the first times I can recall experiencing God's presence.

Another is amid the conifer trees – cedar, spruce, pine – that wrapped a front corner of our home. Exploring under those trees, when I was small enough to fit, was like entering a cave, hidden away. Again, such peace and a presence that was like being hugged and cared for. My love of forests began there.

Later, and for many years, I lived in the Sacramento valley, below the Sierra Nevada Mountains where I spent as much time as possible: hiking, camping, cross-country skiing. Hiking to a fantastic vista and shedding the stresses of life; lunching by a mountain lake; cozy evenings by the ski lodge fireplace, singing with friends; gazing on the stars from the campsite – all these are part of this landscape that still lives deep in my being.

Living in Guelph, Ontario, for many years, I've been formed by stays on Lake Huron. For a week or two at the end of a demanding summer of ministry, I would find the lake taking from me the stresses and fatigue, literally washing them away as I swam. Then she would fill me with peace and renew my creativity and hope. Lake Huron also blessed me one winter. We had had a month of severe cold, and I was grieving the loss of someone dear. I awoke one morning with the notion, unexpectedly, to go to the lake. I had been there many times in summer but never in winter. The idea was strange but so strong, I could not brush it off. Two hours later, I parked the car, bundled up, and walked down the path through the bush… and was gobsmacked. The landscape was like a frozen tundra.

All across the water were icebergs. Two or three rows of them, such that I could see they had formed in stages. It seemed the history of the winter's storms was written in the scene. The beach was also frozen, even in arcs where waves mixed with sand had frozen in motion. I stood in speechless wonder for a long time. It was truly awe-inspiring – an awe that I find within me anew every time I recall that day. Increasing it was the sense that I had been called there, for how else could I understand that wild idea coming unexpectedly? The following week, a thaw came across southern Ontario. Had I not gone to the lake that day, I would have missed it. It was a deep balm for my grieving spirit. Repeatedly, I am healed by nature, renewed in spirit by time in various landscapes.

Each of the sessions in this book will elicit and magnify a different landscape. This first session asks, again: What landscape or landscapes have formed you or touched you deeply? What landscapes have shaped who you are, what you believe, what you love? This session also takes a broad sweep, encompassing the whole cosmos, past, present, and future: God's whole, ongoing creation.

Session 1: What Landscapes Formed Me?

Preparation

* It is helpful to have a table with a candle and a couple of objects from nature, such as some wildflowers, colourful autumn leaves, a seashell, a large attractive stone, a picture of the aurora borealis... This should be visible to the entire group but not dominate. It helps make visible the aim of the retreat but is not the primary focal point; the group itself is that.
* Arrange the group's chairs in a circle; if it is a very large group, you could have two concentric circles, with a break where the facilitator sits so all can see her/him.
* The facilitator will need a watch or clock with second hand and a gentle bell or chime (see Facilitator Guide on page 22).

Welcome by Facilitator (2–3 min.)

* Briefly introduce yourself (1–2 sentences).
* State that you are the facilitator for the program.
* In three or four sentences, summarize the purpose of the retreat and how the session and program will proceed.
* Point out where washrooms are located, invite participants to silence and put away cell phones, and mention any other housekeeping issues.

Opening Prayer (2–3 min.)

Invite the group to pray together for God's grace throughout the retreat. Light the candle on the table you have prepared. Read the following prayer:

We are gathered to gain a deeper appreciation of God and God's creation; to know God and God's creation more fully, more intimately. And so, we pray:

Creator God, Creating God, we ask that you guide our practices over the course of this retreat.

Open our minds and hearts that we may know you
and your creation more fully
and love it more deeply.
Give us trust in you, and in one another.
St. Paul tells us that Christ is your image. In his letter to the Colossians, he writes:

> *Christ is the image of the invisible God, the firstborn of all creation;*
> *for in Christ all things in heaven and on earth were created,*
> *things visible and invisible,*
> *whether thrones or dominions or rulers or powers –*
> *all things have been created through Christ and for Christ.*
> *Christ is before all things, and in Christ all things hold together. (Colossians 1:15-17)*

We pray to open to a new and deeper relationship with your creation, O God.
We pray to see you, Christ, and your creation, more clearly,
to love you more dearly,
and to follow you more nearly.
We ask to be led by you, Holy Spirit.
In the name of the Father, Son, and Holy Spirit. Amen.

Norms (3–4 min.)

Present norms for the group and ask if all can agree to them.

See "Guiding Points for Facilitators" (pages 20–21) for the list of norms.

Introductions by participants (15–20 min., depending on the size of the group)

The facilitator outlines the process for participants and invites them to take the time to offer thoughtful responses rather than rush.

Each person will have 1 to 2 minutes. (It is amazing how much we can say in that time). The facilitator will keep time.

Invite everyone to state three things:

* Your name
* Your desire for your participation in this retreat/program
* Something you love about being alive in Earth[47]

If anyone loses track of time, as we sometimes do, the facilitator calls them back with a gentle bell or chime when it has been 2 minutes; this is to let the speaker know to wrap up that sentence.

Exercise 1: Personal prayer and sharing in small groups (45 min.)

Part A: Personal prayer/reflection in silence (25 min.)

* Find a comfortable place to sit, or walk without disturbing others.
* Begin by asking God for God's presence and guidance in this time of prayer.
* Then ask God for the gift of recalling the significant landscape(s) of your life, especially your early years.
* With God, reflect on the following questions (It's okay if you don't get through all of them. This is prayer, not an exam):
    - What landscape(s) did you grow up in or feel most deeply drawn to?
    - In your mind, picture that landscape. Let it open again in your imagination. Recall how you spent time in it; what creatures you encountered there; what people, if any, you spent time with there.
    - How did you feel about that landscape then? What did you like? What didn't you enjoy?
    - What gifts did it give you?
    - How do you feel about that landscape now?
    - How did it impact your hopes and dreams?
    - How did it shape your personality? … your view of yourself? … your view of the world? …your outlook on life? …your understanding of God?
    - What do you recall now about that landscape that you haven't thought about in a long time?
    - What other landscapes have had a deep impact on you? In what ways? If you have time, reflect further on them as well.
* If you have time at the end, jot a few notes in your journal about what moved you during this time of prayer and recollection.

Part B: Sharing in groups of four (20 min.)*

* Sit in small circles of four. Each person shares, one at a time (4 minutes each), on what moved them in their reflection. This can include sharing about the landscape itself and any of the reflection questions.

* 20 minutes includes 4 minutes per person, plus time to form groups, then return chairs to a large circle at the end.

Break (10 min.)

Exercise 2: Reading and reflection on "The Universe Story" (40 min.)

The story is found at the end of this session.

Invite participants to sit comfortably.

The facilitator reads aloud the introduction and then the story, or they may be divided up among the group ahead of time.

When the story is finished, take a minute or two of silence.

Then share briefly, each offering a word, a phrase, an image that expresses something of your experience or feelings.

Closing Prayer (1 min.)

For your Spirit woven in the fabric of
creation
for the eternal overlapping with time
and the life of earth interlaced with
heaven's vitality
[we] give you thanks, O God.
For your untamed creativity
your boundless mystery
and your passionate yearnings
planted deep in the soul of every human being
[we] give you thanks.
Grant [us] the grace to reclaim these depths
to uncover this treasure
to liberate these longings
and in being set free in [our] own spirits
to act for the well-being of the world.

—J. Philip Newell[48]

Continuing Your Prayer at Home

∗ Praying with My Blessed History

> The life story of each of us can be seen as an experience of the Trinity's love coming to us through the life of Jesus, and through ... friends, family, the living creatures sharing Earth with us, and the actual mineral substances of our earth.[49]

Take some time to gaze over your life, with God, to appreciate all the graced moments, events, and experiences of your life. This is not a thought exercise so much as letting God remind you of various things, people, creatures, events, activities, experiences. Spend time with memories as they arise. Consider especially the ways in which creation has been part of those blessings – through places that have been important or helpful, significant pets or other creatures, a precious tree, perhaps moments such as stargazing, gardening, visiting an especially beautiful place, special meals...

You can do this in a couple of longer prayer times or spend some time with this every day, perhaps considering five or so years at a time.

You can do this while walking, sitting, jogging, gardening...

Afterward, write about it in your journal so you can return to your notes later; or perhaps draw a sort of timeline or make a collage.

∗ Praying with My Rootedness in God

St. Ignatius of Loyola begins his *Spiritual Exercises* with a meditation he calls the Principle and Foundation. The purpose is to begin with some clarity about who God is for me and how I want to orient my life more and more toward God.

Pray with one of these renditions or, after reading them, write your own.

A contemporary rendering of the Principle and Foundation[50]

Lord my God, when Your love spilled over
into creation
You thought of me.
I am
from love   of love   for love.

Let my heart, O God, always
recognize,
cherish,
and enjoy Your goodness in all of creation.

Direct all that is me toward Your praise.
Teach me reverence for every person, all things.
Energize me in Your service.

Lord God,
may nothing ever distract me from Your love…
neither health nor sickness
wealth nor poverty
honor nor dishonor
long life nor short life.

May I never seek nor choose to be other
than You intend or wish.
Amen.

An ecological expression of the Principle and Foundation

As a response to the overflowing love of the Trinity, we humans, in kinship with all other things of the universe, are created to praise, reverence and serve the Trinity in all our life endeavours, and so to discover the fullness of our lives on earth …

In our praising, reverencing and serving the Trinity, we establish a new awareness of connectedness and relationship with all the rest of nature and the need to develop a free loving attitude, even as we use them for our livelihood in all that is left to our free will and is not prohibited. This requires true spiritual freedom on our part. This is the basic attitude toward all of the community of life and is necessary for true love. Such freedom extends to our relationship to everything. So, we need to find this freedom in order to develop a right relationship with creation: human, animal, plants, matter. This gives us the freedom necessary to live with honor or disgrace, in poverty or riches, with a long or short life, in sickness or in health and so of all other matters.[51]

Our one desire is to choose what will better help us be united in love and gratitude with all of creation for the greater praise, reverence and service of the Trinity.[52]

1. Read

* As always, take time to quietly read the opening reflection for the next session. Read it through slowly and attentively. At the end of your reading, let what you have read sift through your mind. What do you still hold as a thought, an emotion, a reaction? What struck you in your reading? What moved you? Note what is stirring in your heart. Jot down some of your thoughts as you prepare for the next session.

2. Suggested viewing and reading

* We highly recommend watching *Journey of the Universe*, an Emmy award–winning, remarkable and inspiring reflection on the human connection to Earth and the cosmos. Narrated by Brian Swimme. 56 minutes. Available on YouTube. There is also a website of the same name with additional resources.
* *Ecology at the Heart of Faith: The Change of Heart that Leads to a New Way of Living on Earth* (Orbis Books, 2008), by diocesan priest Denis Edwards, is a great book to read as you go through this retreat. Edwards was a theologian who wrote for the masses, joining science and faith quite lyrically and yet in uncomplicated terms.
* *My Octopus Teacher*. While recovering from burnout, filmmaker Craig Foster forges an unusual and remarkable friendship with an octopus living in a South African kelp forest. Visiting her every day in the water, he heals and also learns as this animal shares the mysteries of her world. It shows what possibilities there are for our relationship with Earth. This Netflix Original Documentary, released in 2020, won the Oscar for Best Documentary Feature (2021). Available on Netflix and Amazon.
* Some other books that may appeal to you over this retreat:
    - *Earth Prayers from Around the World: 365 Prayers, Poems and Invocations for Honoring the Earth*, ed. Elizabeth Roberts and Elias Amidon (HarperSanFrancisco, 1991).
    - Brian Swimme, *The Universe Is a Green Dragon* (Bear & Company, 2001).
    - Brian Swimme, *The Hidden Heart of the Cosmos* (Orbis Books, 2010).
    - Carolyn W. Toben, *Recovering a Sense of the Sacred: Conversations with Thomas Berry* (Timberlake Earth Sanctuary Press, 2012).

A Telling of *The Universe Story*

compiled by Yvonne Prowse[53]

Introduction

Nature is God's first and primary revelation.

—Thomas Aquinas

God made everything that is made for love;
and the same love sustains everything, and shall do so forever...
God is everything that is good,
and the goodness that is in everything is God.

—Julian of Norwich[54]

We have a beautiful and wonder-filled story of creation in the book of Genesis. We pray with it every year in the Easter Vigil service. (It will also be part of a future session in this retreat.) It tells of God creating the world in six days, then resting, or creating rest, on the seventh day. All through it, we are told that God beheld what God created and saw that it was good. It reveals to us God's creativity and love for us. And yet, as Fr. Denis Edwards, a Catholic theologian, points out, we don't really know *how* exactly God created the world.

A more recent story, a story of the development of the Universe through the understanding of Western science, has been developing now for a few centuries, perhaps beginning in the 16th and 17th centuries, when we realized that Earth is not stationary but moves around the sun. Our knowledge of the details of this story has been developing very rapidly, of late. In the last hundred years or so, we came to know that there are more galaxies than our own Milky Way – a hundred billion more, in fact.

The history of our universe is long – approximately 14 billion years – elaborate, complex, and deeply beautiful. There is so much in it for us to marvel at and to cause us to praise our Creator God. The reading here provides an opportunity to pray with some of the information that science is revealing to us about this extraordinary creation.

Each of us can point to moments of grace in our own unique personal history – moments when the love of God was especially palpable. For example, the moment you were born is an extraordinary, wonderful moment of grace. Our lives are filled with special graces.

So, too, with the story of our universe. It is a long, rich tale of God's love, and we can point to significant moments in it. For example, the moment light began, or the moment eyesight first developed – these are graces worth savouring. The universe story is so involved that various people have outlined it in key moments or events to help us grasp it – moments of grace. This telling is in that mode.

As you listen to this reading, let God reveal the story of the cosmos to you. It is part of your own personal story, and God has a perspective to reveal to you. Tracing our human ancestral lineage has become very popular, as people want to know more of their own early history from before their birth. This is a good way to approach listening to The Universe Story as well. It is indeed our history.

Try not to get too caught up in imagining the timeline itself. Our brains can't really grasp what 14 billion years is. Rather, try to flow with a sense of the passage of time – vast time.

The Story

Begin by imagining being all the way back in time, back before any of what we know existed, back even before the beginning of time, back to when there was only God. And God has a dream and a longing to bring love into form. God is dreaming the world. God is even dreaming you.

> In the beginning was the Word, and the Word was with God, and the Word was God. The Word was in the beginning with God. All things came into being through the Word, and without the Word not one thing came into being. What has come into being in the Word was life, and the life was the light of all people.
>
> (John 1:1-4)

The 1st moment of grace: Some 14 billion years ago, **the universe flares forth**.

Most scientists concur that a tiny fireball, a unique singularity smaller than a grain of sand, yet containing the potential for the entire cosmos, infinitely hot and infinitely condensed, exploded with an immeasurable burst of energy, heat, and light. Scientists can't yet tell what preceded this wondrous flaring forth. However, people of faith know that only God, only absolute love, could generate such energy, and only absolute wisdom could envisage such beauty and harmony.

From that exploding fireball, the universe expanded and cooled with extraordinary speed. Within the first second after this explosion, "ordinary particles such as protons, neutrons and electrons already existed ... By the end of the first three minutes, the observable universe existed as an expanding and cooling fireball, made up of the nuclei of hydrogen and helium. [Edwards, *Ecology at the Heart of Faith*, 8]

The 2nd moment of grace: A billion or two years later, **galaxies, including our Milky Way, emerge**.

As the universe continued to cool and expand, atoms were formed and, over the course of millions of years, the force of gravity. This force of attraction condensed matter into stars, which clustered into galaxies. Nuclear reactions started up again in these first-generation stars when they collapsed with tremendous explosion – a supernova – spewing out the heavier elements of carbon and iron, elements essential for life.

Crab Nebula, M1, NGC 1952. Photo by NASA Hubble Space Telescope (Hubblesite.org)

The 3rd moment: Eons pass as stars continue to form and eventually explode. One of these is our grandmother star; her life ended about 4.6 to 5 billion years ago in **a supernova that gives rise to our star, the Sun**.

Can we stretch our imaginations to try to get a sense of the immensity of the universe? Our own medium-sized galaxy contains some 200 billion stars. It takes light 100,000 years to cross from one side of our galaxy to the other. Mingled in with the stars are vast clouds of dust and gas, the material from which future stars will be made. Now consider that there are over 300 billion galaxies in the universe.

The 4th moment: At various distances from the Sun, large segments of matter clustered together. Their rotational fields attracted more matter, which coalesced, **forming planets, including our planet, Earth**, which is about 4.5 billion years old.

The 5th moment: About 4.1 billion years ago, Earth began as a ball of molten rock, which gradually cooled. As volcanoes continued to expel hot magma to the surface, steam condensed above. Torrential rains from the moist atmosphere formed rivers and great seas as **water covered the earth**.

The 6th moment: Earth was just the right size and the right distance from the Sun to allow the evolution of life to begin. The great seas were a rich chemical brew in which emerged the **astounding miracle of the first living cell**, about 4 billion years ago. That first single cell held the potential for all life on Earth. Then cells began to divide and multiply into tiny creatures in the sea.

The 7th moment: These miniscule bacteria in the sea invented ways to capture energy from the sun to use as food. In the process, they gave off oxygen. Dominican sister Miriam MacGillis suggests that this process of **photosynthesis** was the first transubstantiation.

The 8th moment: Around 1 billion years ago, cells became attracted to each other and connected to form ever more complex life forms **through the sexual reproduction of early cells**. It can be valuable to recognize this as God's creative action. You could say that this is the dynamic of divine creative love. The Jesuit scientist and mystic Pierre Teilhard de Chardin notes that the dynamic of this ongoing evolutionary process is attraction-connection-complexity and, eventually, consciousness.

The 9th moment: As life continued to diversify in the seas and become more complex, **eyesight** developed. Earth saw herself for the first time. Soft-bodied animals began to evolve. Over the next 70 million years, shells, jaws, beaks, and skeletons developed.

The 10th moment: Eventually, there was enough accumulation of oxygen to form Earth's ozone layer, providing protection from the harmful ultraviolet rays of the sun. It was then safe for life to creep out of the water and colonize the surface of the Earth. Worms, mollusks, and crustaceans left the water and breathed air. **The first gymnosperms – seed-producing plants – evolved** (425 million years ago).

The 11th moment: We jump forward to the time of the dinosaurs and flowers (235 million years ago). They flourished for about 170 million years. Dinosaurs developed parental care: some stayed with their young after they hatched, nurturing them toward independence. Flowers evolved with an array of colours, perfumes, and delightful nectars.

The 12th moment: As foreleg bones gradually evolved into wing bones, and jawbones into beaks, and scales into feathers, **birds emerged** about 150 million years ago.

The 13th moment: A short time later, cosmologically speaking, **marsupial mammals evolved** (125 million years ago). They don't develop a placenta in the womb and therefore give birth to their young after a short gestation period, then carry them in an external pouch.

The 14th moment: About 67 million years ago, it seems **huge asteroids collided with earth**, causing the extinction of the dinosaurs. Small mammals quickly took up the available ecological niches, and primates appeared.

The 15th moment: This ushered in the Cenozoic Era, a time of amazing creativity in which mammalian life blossomed… an era that lasted until only the most recent centuries. Approximately 200,000 years ago, as mammalian life diversified and multiplied, a particular mammal emerged into the fold: ***Homo sapiens***.

The 16th moment: As humans developed, **Indigenous societies and primal worship** emerged (40,000 years ago). **Agricultural societies** began (9,000 years ago). And the **world's religions**, such as Judaism, began to develop (6,000 years ago).

The 17th moment: While it is not part of the scientific story, we note an extraordinary moment 2,000 years ago: **the incarnation of Christ**. God become flesh… *sarx*, in Greek. "The flesh that the Word became is part of the vast body of the cosmos," says theologian Elizabeth Johnson. "The Word of God entered into solidarity not only with all humanity but also with the whole biophysical world. Hence, the incarnation, a densely specific expression of the love of God already poured out in creation, confers dignity on the whole of earthly reality."[55]

The 18th moment: **The rise of modern science** began very recently, just 500 or so years ago. With it came the revelation that Earth is not the centre of the universe.

The 19th moment: In the last 300 years, there have been amazing advancements in medical science, and human life expectancy overall increased significantly. However, the Cenozoic age declined with another period of **mass extinction of species**, this time **caused by human activity**.

The 20th moment: In 1966 and again in 1968, with space travel, **we humans saw Earth from space** for the first time. Can we bring our imaginations to that image? Earth appearing like a blue marble against the vast background of space. Now see in your imagination that under Earth's shielding atmosphere there exists the whole network of living creatures that have evolved,

> from wee microorganisms to giant sequoias and massive blue whales, including humans toward the larger end of the scale, all interacting with the land, water and air of their different ecosystems. In scientific terms this enveloping skein of life is called the biosphere. In faith terms it is called the community of creation. Picture yourself as an indigenous member of this community that all comes from the hand of the one gracious God who created everything out of love. Not only that, but throughout time every creature with its relationships is held in existence by the same vivifying Giver of Life. At the end, all will be gathered into a new heaven and a new earth by the same divine, ineffable love.[56]

This Present Moment of Grace: Now come into the present moment – this current moment of grace. Rest. Breathe. Be aware of your body sitting in the chair. Consider the story you have just heard. What do you feel? What did you experience about God? … about the Universe? … about Earth? What has moved you most in this story? … Is there an image or a phrase that stands out for you or expresses your experience of this story?

Session 2

Water

Opening Reflection

Trevor Scott, SJ

The Fragile Gift of Water in Our Lives

A special place within the abundance of natural beauty of North America captured the visual imagination of one artist, giving it iconic status: Lake Superior. It is as if Lawren Harris, one of the Group of Seven Canadian painters, rendered the scriptural imagination of Genesis: "God's Spirit brooded like a bird above the watery abyss." Looking at Harris's *Morning, Lake Superior*, you feel as if you are gazing upon this Spirit of God from the beginning of time hovering and stirring over our watery womb of life. Water, in the form of Harris's Lake Superior, has an ethereal, other-worldly, sublime presence... as if portraying God's very presence.

Along the hiking trails above Lake Superior between Sault Ste. Marie and Wawa, Ontario, which I hike every year, I feel that I am walking in Lawren Harris's footsteps, seeing and absorbing what he saw over a century earlier. Despite the distance of time between my era and his, this special spot in our world remains the same, eternally blessed and seemingly untouched, in large part thanks to the stewardship of Lake Superior Provincial Park. To walk the shores and shoreline hills of Lake Superior today, one is overwhelmed by the freshness of it all, by the abundance of all this fresh, cool water.

Lawren S. Harris, *Morning, Lake Superior*
Used with permission of The Montreal Museum of Fine Arts.
Photo credit: The Montreal Museum of Fine Arts, Brian Merrett.

The local Ojibwe people referred to this great body of water as *Gitchee Gumee*, "shining Big Sea." The French called it *le lac supérieur* because it was the largest and deepest, by far, of the Great Lakes. But also because of its northernmost position among them and its great height hovering over them all, feeding its abundance to them through their natural river systems – Niagara Falls, most imaginatively – and shipping canals built over the last century and a half. This aspect of the generous and shimmering abundance of Lake Superior waters can remind us of God's own fruitful abundance in the imagery of Isaiah 44:3… "For I will pour water on the thirsty land, and streams on the dry ground; I will pour my spirit on your descendants, and my blessing on your offspring." Lake Superior can have that effect upon its visitors through its sublime, divine-like presence.

But make no doubt, despite its 'superior' disposition, Lake Superior, like all lakes, like all rivers, even the enveloping oceans and seas themselves, is fragile. We cannot take the presence of our waters for granted. Large portions of Lake Erie are often filled with life-choking algae blooms birthed from agricultural chemical run-offs. The lakes of California and rivers of Texas have been evaporating at staggering rates, and even been fully parched, through droughts because of climate change. We can see the potential devastation of our disappearing waters on our planetary neighbour, the red planet Mars. Even if this is our own planet's natural destiny in the eons to come, do we really want to help speed up this evolutionary destiny for our future generations?

One dramatic example of the fragility of our waters and our role in their diminishment is the Aral Sea, located between Kazakhstan and Uzbekistan. It was once considered the fourth-largest lake in the world. But beginning in the 1960s, with Soviet irrigation projects that diverted the rivers feeding the Aral Sea, it eventually shrank to 10% of its size. What was once the eastern lakebed of the Aral Sea is now called the Aralkum Desert and is seeded with life-threatening industrial chemicals.

Evolution of the Aral Sea (Kazakhstan-Uzbekistan) (NASA. Collage by Producercunningham, Public domain, via Wikimedia Commons)

Our brokenness as human beings, our inadequacy to reverently hold and respond to the abundance of life all around and within us without the grace of our Creator, is what leads us toward our own unintended creations… the parched, chemical-laden deserts of our world that once held the wombs of life. Jeremiah rightly reminds us of our brokenness and destructive capacities: "For my people have committed two evils: they have forsaken me, the fountain of living water, and dug out cisterns for themselves, cracked cisterns that can hold no water" (Jeremiah 2:13).

But the gospel message reminds us of our capacity for resurrection. The public ministry of Christ in communion with his disciples begins on the shores of the shimmering Lake Galilee, a small, fragile lake teeming with life within the encroaching desert of the Holy Land. Was it a coincidence of history that Jesus was raised upon and began his life's work on the shores of Lake Galilee, between lake and desert? The gospel story draws our attention to the desert of the Cross by first drawing our attention to water itself: the material beginning of our lives within amniotic fluid and the spiritual beginnings of our lives with our baptism, our life in the Spirit of God.

Sea of Galillee (Shutterstock / Max Shamota)

Ghost ships Aral Sea (Kazakhstan-Uzbekistan) (Sebastian Kluger, CC BY-SA 3.0 <https://creativecommons.org/licenses/by-sa/3.0>, via Wikimedia Commons)

Session 2: Water

Preparation

* Video: Archbishop Justin Welby on Prince George's Christening (available on YouTube)
* Large bowl of water plus towels
* Background audio: Flowing water

Opening Prayer (3 min.)

For Our Earth[57]

All-powerful God, you are present in the whole universe and in the smallest of your creatures.
You embrace with your tenderness all that exists.

Pour out upon us the power of your love,
that we may protect life and beauty.

Fill us with peace, that we may live
as brothers and sisters, harming no one.

O God of the poor,
help us to rescue the abandoned and forgotten of this earth, so precious in your eyes.

Bring healing to our lives,
that we may protect the world and not prey on it,
that we may sow beauty, not pollution and destruction.

Touch the hearts
of those who look only for gain
at the expense of the poor and the earth.

Teach us to discover the worth of each thing,
to be filled with awe and contemplation,
to recognize that we are profoundly united
with every creature as we journey towards your infinite light.

We thank you for being with us each day.

Encourage us, we pray, in our struggle
for justice, love and peace. Amen.

(2 minutes of silent reflection)

Protecting the Oceans

In tropical and subtropical seas, we find coral reefs comparable to the great forests on dry land, for they shelter approximately a million species, including fish, crabs, molluscs, sponges and algae. Many of the world's coral reefs are already barren or in a state of constant decline. "Who turned the wonderworld of the seas into underwater cemeteries bereft of colour and life?" This phenomenon is due largely to pollution which reaches the sea as the result of deforestation, agricultural monocultures, industrial waste and destructive fishing methods, especially those using cyanide and dynamite. It is aggravated by the rise in temperature of the oceans. All of this helps us to see that every intervention in nature can have consequences which are not immediately evident, and that certain ways of exploiting resources prove costly in terms of degradation which ultimately reaches the ocean bed itself. (*Laudato Si'* #41)

Group Sharing (10 min.)

Pope Francis draws our attention to the intimate connection between the impacts upon the environment and their effects on our interpersonal relationships… the cry of the Earth leads to the cry of the impoverished and marginalized. In turn, the healing of the Earth can more readily lead to healing with our neighbours.

Choose one question to share:

1. What image or sentiment resonated more with you in this opening prayer?
2. In your experience, how have you associated care for Creation as intimately connected with pastoral care with those around you, particularly the impoverished and marginalized?

Exercise 1: Genesis 1 (15 min.)

Read the following text aloud in the large-group setting, taking turns. (5 min.)

Genesis 1[58]

Heaven and Earth

1-2
First this: God created the Heavens and Earth—all you see, all you don't see. Earth was a soup of nothingness, a bottomless emptiness, an inky blackness. God's Spirit brooded like a bird above the watery abyss.

3-5
God spoke: "Light!"
And light appeared.
God saw that light was good
and separated light from dark.
God named the light Day,
he named the dark Night.
It was evening, it was morning—
Day One.

6-8
God spoke: "Sky! In the middle of the waters;
separate water from water!"
God made sky.
He separated the water under sky
from the water above sky.
And there it was:
he named sky the Heavens;
It was evening, it was morning—
Day Two.

9-10
God spoke: "Separate!
Water-beneath-Heaven, gather into one place;
Land, appear!"
And there it was.
God named the land Earth.
He named the pooled water Ocean.
God saw that it was good.

11-13
God spoke: "Earth, green up! Grow all varieties
of seed-bearing plants,
Every sort of fruit-bearing tree."
And there it was.
Earth produced green seed-bearing plants,
all varieties,
And fruit-bearing trees of all sorts.
God saw that it was good.
It was evening, it was morning—
Day Three.

14-15
God spoke: "Lights! Come out!
Shine in Heaven's sky!
Separate Day from Night.
Mark seasons and days and years,
Lights in Heaven's sky to give light to Earth."
And there it was.

16-19
God made two big lights, the larger
to take charge of Day,
The smaller to be in charge of Night;
and he made the stars.
God placed them in the heavenly sky
to light up Earth
And oversee Day and Night,
to separate light and dark.

Water as a Basic and Universal Human Right

Our world has a grave social debt towards the poor who lack access to drinking water, because *they are denied the right to a life consistent with their inalienable dignity.* This debt can be paid partly by an increase in funding to provide clean water and sanitary services among the poor. But water continues to be wasted, not only in the developed world but also in developing countries which possess it in abundance. This shows that the problem of water is partly an educational and cultural issue, since there is little awareness of the seriousness of such behavior within a context of great inequality. (*Laudato Si'* #30)

God saw that it was good.
It was evening, it was morning—
Day Four.

20-23
God spoke: "Swarm, Ocean, with fish and all sea life!
Birds, fly through the sky over Earth!"
God created the huge whales,
all the swarm of life in the waters,
And every kind and species of flying birds.
God saw that it was good.
God blessed them: "Prosper! Reproduce! Fill Ocean!
Birds, reproduce on Earth!"
It was evening, it was morning—
Day Five.

24-25
God spoke: "Earth, generate life! Every sort and kind:
cattle and reptiles and wild animals—all kinds."
And there it was:
wild animals of every kind,
Cattle of all kinds, every sort of reptile and bug.
God saw that it was good.

26-28
God spoke: "Let us make human beings in our image, make them
reflecting our nature
So they can be responsible for the fish in the sea,
the birds in the air, the cattle,
And, yes, Earth itself,
and every animal that moves on the face of Earth."
God created human beings;
he created them godlike,
Reflecting God's nature.
He created them male and female.
God blessed them:
"Prosper! Reproduce! Fill Earth! Take charge!
Be responsible for fish in the sea and birds in the air,
for every living thing that moves on the face of Earth."

29-30
Then God said, "I've given you
every sort of seed-bearing plant on Earth
And every kind of fruit-bearing tree,
given them to you for food.
To all animals and all birds,
everything that moves and breathes,
I give whatever grows out of the ground for food."
And there it was.

31
God looked over everything he had made;
it was so good, so very good!
It was evening, it was morning—
Day Six.

Protecting the Oceans

Let us also mention the system of governance of the oceans. International and regional conventions do exist, but fragmentation and the lack of strict mechanisms of regulation, control and penalization end up undermining these efforts. The growing problem of marine waste and the protection of the open seas represent particular challenges. What is needed, in effect, is an agreement on systems of governance for the whole range of so-called "global commons". (*Laudato Si'* #174)

(2 minutes of silent reflection)

Group Sharing (10 min.)

Choose one question to share:

1. Imagine yourself at the very beginning of time, entering the desire of the Creator to create. Where do you feel this desire of God to create comes from?

2. Why do you feel creation would begin from a watery abyss? What is it about the value and meaning of water that would make it the womb of God's Creation?
3. Could you imagine God's Creation without the presence of water? What could Creation look like without water?

Exercise 2: Contemplation (5 min.)

Contemplate this NASA image of our water-filled planet in silence for a few minutes.

Earth straddling limb of moon (NASA/Goddard/Arizona State University)

Group Sharing (15 min.)

Choose one question to share:

1. What struck you most in this image of our home planet from the perspective of the Moon?
2. Do you find yourself drawn to the desolate beauty of the Moon, looking at the fragile beauty of our world from afar? How?
3. What do the terrifying extremes of the lifeless world of the Moon evoke in you? Does it help you appreciate our water-covered world?
4. Does this perspective of our world help you more deeply appreciate how intimately our lives are sustained by water, especially in contrast to the Sahara Desert of northern Africa?
5. Contemplating the beauty of our world from the perspective of deep space, with no sign of political boundaries or demarcations, how does it change your attitude toward Creation, the environment of all our social and political strife and scars, as well as all of our love and care?

Break (10 min.)

Exercise 3: Water Scarcity (15 min.)

Read aloud the following facts as a large group, taking turns.

Water Scarcity[59]

* Water covers about 71% of the Earth.
* 96.5% of all Earth's water is from the ocean.
* Only 2.5% of all our planet's water is drinkable fresh water.
* Only 1% of all our freshwater is easily accessible, such as in rivers and lakes. The rest of this 1% is frozen in glaciers.
* About 2 billion people worldwide do not have access to safe drinking water.
* Roughly half of the world's population is experiencing severe water scarcity for at least part of the year (Intergovernmental Panel on Climate Change [IPCC]). These numbers are expected to increase, exacerbated by

Where Water Stress Will Be Highest by 2050

Projected ratio of human water demand to water availability (water stress level) in 2050*

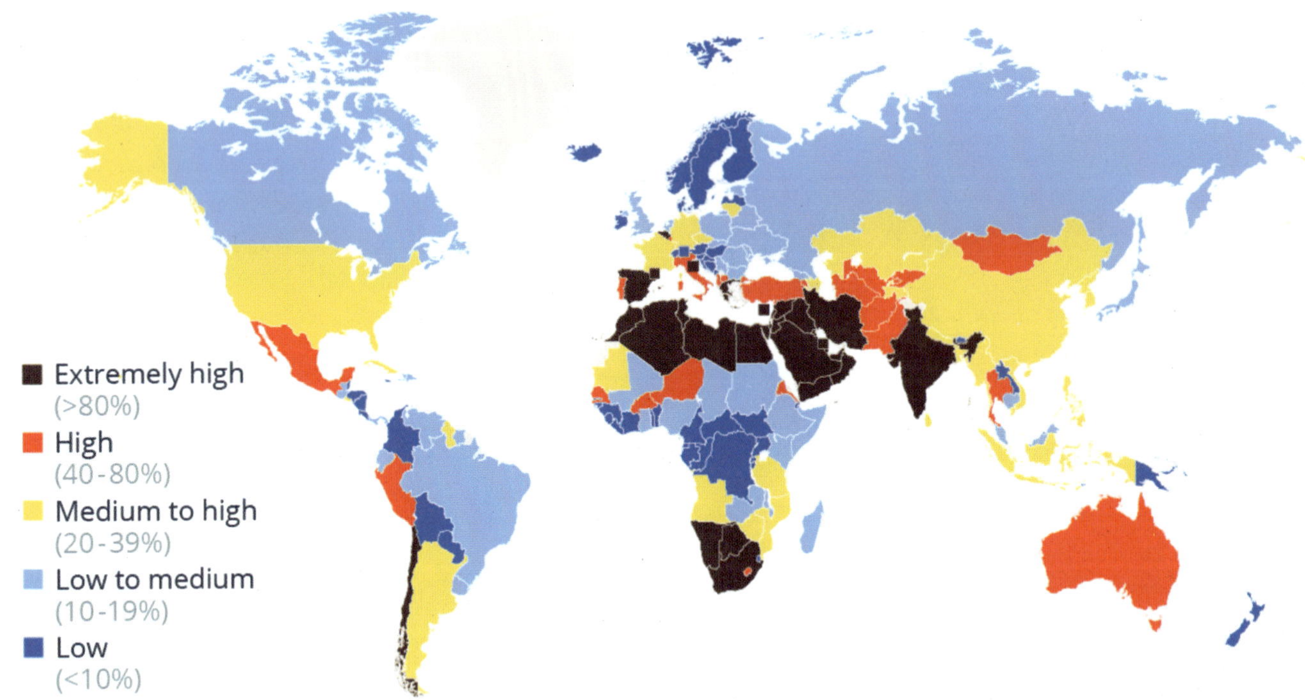

* According to "business as usual" scenario=middle-of-the-road future where temperatures increase by 2.8°C to 4.6°C by 2100

Source: World Resources Institute

Where water stress will be highest by 2050 (https://www.statista.com/chart/26140/water-stress-projections-global)

climate change and population growth (World Meteorological Organization).

* Water supplies stored in glaciers and snow cover are projected to further decline over the course of this century, reducing water availability during warm and dry periods in regions supplied by meltwater from major mountain ranges, where more than one sixth of the world's population currently live (IPCC).

* Sea-level rise is projected to extend salinization of groundwater, decreasing freshwater availability for humans and ecosystems in coastal areas (IPCC).

* Climate change, population growth, and increasing water scarcity will put pressure on food supply (IPCC) as most of the freshwater used, about 70% on average, is used for agriculture (it takes between 2,000 and 5,000 litres of

water to produce a person's daily food) (Food and Agriculture Organization).

The Lower Mainland (British Columbia) is probably the most diked jurisdiction in Canada. It's also where juvenile salmon come through on their way out of the Fraser River into the Salish Sea. They need the small side channels, tributaries, and sluices along the Fraser to over-winter in and to learn how to hunt and feed, so that when they get to the ocean, they have the best possible chance of life... when the river splays out through the Lower Mainland, you start to see more embankments, to smell the manure put on the fields, to see a sheen on the water from a runoff.

You start to see how slowly, over time, we have degraded this waterway. We never think about it as a whole—we break it into pieces. We give permits for this or licenses for that: "Let's remove some trees here. It's not a big deal."

—Lina Azeez, Campaign Manager,
Connected Water,
Watershed Watch Salmon Society
(Vancouver, BC)[60]

Water Hazards[61]

* Climate change has made extreme weather events such as floods and droughts more likely and more severe (IPCC).

* Rising global temperatures increase the moisture the atmosphere can hold, resulting in more storms and heavy rains, but also more intense dry spells as more water evaporates from the land and global weather patterns change (World Bank).

* The frequency of heavy precipitation events will likely increase over most areas during the 21st century, with more rain-generated floods. At the same time, the proportion of land in extreme drought at any one time is also projected to increase (IPCC).

* Water-related disasters have dominated the list of disasters over the past 50 years and account for 70% of all deaths related to natural disasters (World Bank).

Forty years ago, after meeting my husband, Gary, we set off in a canoe from the salt water on the Atlantic side and paddled the canoe up the St. Lawrence and through the Great Lakes. We went upstream and downstream, across watersheds, to take us all the way to the salt water up in the northwest.

Journeying on water connected us to the flow of the land and to the people who lived in many different places. Having this time to journey gave me a very "in my bones" connection to water as a flowing being on the land that the water connects. As you cross watersheds, you're flowing with the water down into the next lake.

—Joanie McGuffin, Executive Director,
Lake Superior Watershed Conservancy,
author and explorer (Goulais River, Ontario)[62]

Water Solutions[63]

* Healthy aquatic ecosystems and improved water management can lower greenhouse gas emissions and provide protection against climate hazards (Water and Climate Coalition).

* Wetlands such as mangroves, seagrasses, marshes, and swamps are highly effective carbon sinks that absorb and store CO2, helping to reduce greenhouse gas emissions (UN Environment Programme [UNEP]).

* Wetlands also serve as a buffer against extreme weather events (UNEP). They provide a natural shield against storm surges and absorb excess water and precipitation. Through the plants and microorganisms they house, wetlands also provide water storage and purification.

* Climate-smart agriculture using drip irrigation and other means of using water more

efficiently can help reduce demand on freshwater supplies (UNEP).

> Water is living. When you talk to water, it's in our spirit that those conversations happen, in our heart. When you're talking to water, you're not only talking to water, you're talking to everything that's in the water and everything that's around the water.
>
> –Jesse Cardinal, Executive Director, Keepers of the Water (Kikino Métis Settlement, Alberta)[64]

(2 minutes of silent reflection)

Protecting the Oceans

Oceans not only contain the bulk of our planet's water supply, but also most of the immense variety of living creatures, many of them still unknown to us and threatened for various reasons. What is more, marine life in rivers, lakes, seas and oceans, which feeds a great part of the world's population, is affected by uncontrolled fishing, leading to a drastic depletion of certain species. Selective forms of fishing which discard much of what they collect continue unabated. Particularly threatened are marine organisms which we tend to overlook, like some forms of plankton; they represent a significant element in the ocean food chain, and species used for our food ultimately depend on them. (*Laudato Si'* 40)

Exercise 4: Group Sharing (15 min.)

Choose one or two questions to share:

1. What struck you most from these observations of both the fragility and blessing of water?
2. Which fact or insight surprised you the most?
3. Have you ever experienced or lived in a region of our world with limited clean water?
4. How did you cope? What solutions were you a part of or witness to?
5. Do you see water as a living being and not just a container of living beings? If as a living being, do you feel water should deserve all the legal protections of living beings, such as human beings and animals?
6. Have you understood and appreciated water as a continually flowing ecosystem throughout our entire world, as one interconnected, flowing body? If so, how does this perspective affect your relationship with the water in your own neighbourhood?
7. Have you ever been an agent of stopping this bodily flow of water in your own region… of degrading the waterways, of breaking it up into pieces? Did it lead to fruitfulness or unintended destructive consequences, seen or unseen?

Exercise 5: Water Is Life (20 min.)

Watch Archbishop Justin Welby on Prince George's Christening (5 min.).

Water Ritual Activity (15 min.)

1. Preparation

Set out a large bowl full of water.

Have the sound of gently flowing water audible in the background.

2. Reflection

Water is a source of life.

* Silently reflect on the importance of water in your own life.
* Think about how it might represent God's presence.

RECONCILING GOD, CREATION AND HUMANITY:

ECOLOGICAL EXAMEN

In *Laudato Si'* Pope Francis asked us to care for creation and to reconcile our relationship with God, creation and one another. Borrowing from the great Ignatian tradition of examens, this *Ecological Examen* asks you to reflect on your personal relationship with creation, to acknowledge and amend your ways and to promote ecological justice by standing in solidarity with those most impacted by environmental harm.

Developed by St. Ignatius Loyola, the *Examen* is a technique of prayerful reflection on the events of the day in order to detect God's presence and discern his direction for us.

Begin the Examen by placing yourself or your group in a posture that allows you to be open to the ways the Spirit is working in you. There are six steps in the Examen:

GRATITUDE

I give thanks to God for creation and for being wonderfully made.

(Where did I feel God's presence in creation today?)

AWARENESS

I ask for the grace to see creation as God does – in all its splendor and suffering.

(Do I see the beauty of creation and hear the cries of the earth and the poor?)

UNDERSTANDING

I ask for the grace to look closely to see how my life choices impact creation and the poor and vulnerable.

(What challenges or joys do I experience as I recall my care for creation? How can I turn away from a throwaway culture and instead stand in solidarity with creation and the poor?)

CONVERSION

I ask for the grace of conversion towards ecological justice and reconciliation.

(Where have I fallen short in caring for creation and my brothers and sisters? How do I ask for a conversion of heart?)

RECONCILIATION

I ask for the grace to reconcile my relationship with God, creation, and humanity and to stand in solidarity through my actions.

(How can I repair my relationship with creation and make choices consistent with my desire for reconciliation with creation?)

PRAYER

I offer a closing prayer for the earth and the vulnerable in our society.

ecoexamen.org

Ecological Examen (Ignatian Solidarity Network, Jesuits, ecoexamen.org)

3. Action

- ✳ In pairs, pour fresh water over each other's hands, experiencing the flow of the water over your hands together.
- ✳ As you are pouring water over each other's hands, offer a silent prayer for the other person: e.g., "May you be blessed with the abundance and freshness of God's ever-flowing Creation."

4. Silent Reflection

- ✳ What memories come to mind as you feel the water?
- ✳ Baptism? Your baptism? Jesus' baptism?
- ✳ Jesus washing the feet of others?
- ✳ Washing your hands before a special meal?
- ✳ Washing your hands after working hard with your hands?

Closing Prayer: Ecological Examen[65] (10 min.)

Together in a large-group setting, silently ponder each point of the Ecological Examen on age 43.

Designate one or several persons to gently read aloud each point of the Examen, with adequate pauses in between for everyone to have the space to silent reflect: about 2 minutes for each Examen point.

Continuing Your Prayer at Home

- ✳ When you take your morning shower or bath, and when you drink a fresh glass of water, pause for a prayerful moment of thanksgiving that you live in a country so blessed with clean, readily accessible water for most people.
- ✳ Watch the 2012 NFB documentary *The People of the Kattawapiskak River*, by Indigenous filmmaker Alanis Obomsawin: https://www.nfb.ca/film/people_of_kattawapiskak_river/ This documentary reveals the ongoing crisis of the lack of fresh water, along with other infrastructures, within a northern Indigenous community that most places in Canada take for granted.
- ✳ Wander through *Mind the Water Gap: Mapping the World's Water Shortages* on the National Geographic website, on the precarious nature of water in our world.[66]
- ✳ Take time to quietly read the opening reflection for Session 3: Mountains. Read it slowly and attentively. At the end of your reading, let what you have read sift through your mind. What do you still hold as a thought, an emotion, a reaction? What struck you in your reading? What moved you? Note what is stirring in your heart. Jot down some of your thoughts as you prepare for the next session.

Water as a Basic and Universal Human Right

Even as the quality of available water is constantly diminishing, in some places there is a growing tendency, despite its scarcity, to privatize this resource, turning it into a commodity subject to the laws of the market. Yet *access to safe drinkable water is a basic and universal human right, since it is essential to human survival and, as such, is a condition for the exercise of other human rights.* (*Laudato Si'* #30)

Session 3

Mountains

Opening Reflection

Yvonne Prowse

Big Valley Bluff. An obscure, little-known place down an unpaved, well-rutted logging road. I happened upon it one day when I was longing to clear my mind and heart of current burdens, seeking a sense of God's presence in nature. Driving along the four-lane highway, I noticed a small, very plain road marker with the enticing name. I impulsively turned off the highway, hoping that what nudged me might be the Holy Spirit leading me.

When I reached the bluff, there were no buildings, not even a sign. The vista was its own marker. Across a deep, broad valley was a range of mountains – some nearer, some farther – creating layers of hills and summits under a vast sky. In the deep valley below me, I watched turkey vultures and hawks glide on the breeze and ride the updrafts. I could see small rapids in the river way down below, too far for me to be able to hear the water. But I listened to the breezes in their various forms. Slightly haunting down in the valley; akin to ocean waves as they gently swept through the pines and spruce trees; cleansig and refreshing as they brushed my ears. And the clean mountain-forest air; that alone made me breathe easier. The fact that logging was obviously occurring nearby – and not logging done in concert with the life of the forest – did not mar the experience. Rather, it kept it grounded in the reality of our world that is filled with amazing grace that somehow manages to encompass deep sorrows.

Despite my preference for hiking when I am out in the mountains, I visited this bluff many times for a couple of years. I would soak in the beauty and peace and be refreshed. It was around that time that I also started learning various poems by heart so I could take them with me on the trail.

One of the first, and still a favourite, expresses my experience of spiritual and emotional renewal.

> *My help is in the mountain*
> *where I take myself to heal...*
> *I find a rock with sun on it*
> *and a stream where the water runs gentle*
> *and the trees which one by one give me company....*
> *—Nancy C. Wood*[67]

I am fortunate that all my life, I have found that getting into nature – be that the wilderness, or a walk by the river running through town – grounds me, heals me, uplifts me. But the mountains resonate in my soul in a unique way. A couple of years ago, while recovering from a long and debilitating illness, I drove across the continent to get to the high desert of the Colorado Plateau, at the western base of the Rockies. Crossing the state of Colorado, as I finally caught my first glimpse of the Rocky

Mountains, I was moved to tears. It was not just their majestic beauty but something of how they wrapped my pain and longing, perhaps because of how my body holds the memories of the spiritual freedom and solace the many hikes I have made have given me.

This is not everyone's experience of mountains. A client recently spoke of feeling daunted and a bit too overwhelmed by the Rocky Mountains. She finds them unsettling. And mountain ranges themselves vary. The primarily deciduous forests and lower peaks of the Appalachian range do not stir me as deeply as the granite crags and conifers of the Sierra Nevada … where Big Valley Bluff is.

Getting into the higher elevations is part of it. And looking out across the peaks. I have had many opportunities to hike river gorges. But that means the work of hiking up came at the end of the journey. Hiking up Horsetail Falls in the Desolation Wilderness means a good workout for the first couple of hours, with rests all along the falling river, shedding the stress and strain of the week, to then lunch at an expansive view at the top of the falls. The return hike is lighter in so many ways – physical, emotional, spiritual.

Of course, my experience is as a visitor: a tourist, really. I try to imagine the lives of people who live in and of the mountains. I am thinking of the intimacy with the land that people in remote villages in the Himalayas have. Including the sherpa, who risk their lives daily to eke out a living through brute strength as guides and human pack mules for Western mountaineers. But these people also know the life of the mountains in their blood. They know what shifting winds and changes in clouds mean for the weather. They know where, in which seasons, to find water; where and when edible plants grow; and how much they can take while still allowing the plants to thrive. One of my favourite movies is *The Eagle Huntress*, a documentary of a 13-year-old girl born into seven generations of male eagle hunters in the Altai Mountains of Mongolia. With te support and training of her father, but going against sexist traditions, she becomes the first female eagle hunter to compete in the annual Golden Eagle Festival. The movie also shows the family's tandem lives – living in town and attending school in winter, and living as nomads in the Altai the rest of the year in a deep intimacy with the land. And it tells much of the lives of the eagles and the reverence of the Kazakh people for them.

Mountains are so much more than the rocky uplifts of earth. And they are far more than places that need to exist for humans' solace, pleasure, or resources. They are living landscapes, full of unique plant, animal, insect, and microbe lives that mak up vital ecosystems in Earth's life. Their glaciers and snowpack are also vital water sources for all life. Yet, they are seriously under threat, due to the warming climate, human development, and resource extraction. While we were preparing this book, the Canadian Mountain Assessment[68] was released. It is a first-of-its-kind publication that joins Western academic and Indigenous knowledge, with over 80 contributors. The attractive work discusses the biophysical characteristics of mountains, mountains as homelands, the gift of mountains to human well-being, and mountains under pressure; finally, it addresses desirable mountain futures. They tell us that one quarter of Canada is covered in mountainous terrain, making Canada the fourth most mountainous country in the world. One third of Canada's pecies at risk of extinction rely on mountain ecosystems. Many plants and animals are found only in those regions. And some may not persist if our ecological crises continue.[69]

These facts are not news to most of us. So, they beg questions of how we process and hold the information; how we hold mountains themselves in our hearts and minds; and what our faith in the Creating Trinity leads us to in relation to mountains.

Session 3: Mountains

Preparation

* Fill a basket with stones – at least two per participant. A second basket for half the stones will be needed throughout the remainder of the retreat program.
* Choose music for several moments where music is suggested.

Welcome (5 min.)

The facilitator warmly welcomes the group.

* If the group is still learning one another's names, go around the circle with each person saying their name, and the group repeating it back with "Welcome, _(name)__."

Opening Prayer (20 min.)

Praise and Thaksgiving

* Play the Bob Dufford hymn "Sing to the Mountains"[70] or another suitable song.
* Have three different members of the group read the three passages below, with a short pause for silence after each.

From the Book of Amos:

For lo, the one who forms the mountains,
creates the wind,
reveals his thoughts to mortals,
makes the morning darkness,
and treads on the heights of the earth—
the Lord, the God of Hosts, is his name!
(Amos 4:13)

From *Laudato Si'*:

The entire material universe speaks of God's love, his boundless affection for us. Soil, water, mountains: everything is, as it were, a caress of God. … God has written a precious book, "whose letters are the multitude of created things present in the universe."[71] The Canadian bishops rightly pointed out that no creature is excluded from this manifestation of God: "From panoramic vistas to the tiniest living form, nature is a constant source of wonder and awe. It is also a continuing revelation of the divine."[72] (Laudato Si' #84, 85))

From the Book of Isaiah:

How beautiful upon the mountains are the feet of the messenger who announces peace. (Isaiah 52:7)

Invite the group to sit in prayerful silence together, reflecting on what they are grateful for: from this day, the past week, in their personal life, in the greater world…

After 2 to 3 minutes (ring a chime to denote the transition), invite people to share briefly why they are grateful. They might voice one thing or three or four.

Rocky Mountains, Alberta, Canada (Yvonne Prowse)

Exercise 1: Litany of Mountains

(5 min.)

The following litany is to be read aloud, with a different reader for each section.

a. Rocky Mountains of Alberta
   Torngat Mountains of Labrador
   Coast Mountains of British Columbia
   Saint Elias Mountains of Yukon
   Mackenzie Mountains of the Northwest Territories

   Considered by many to be Earth's most striking features, mountains cover a quarter of Earth's land surface.

b. The Himalayas, Atlas, Andes, Appalachians, Alps, Sierra Nevada, Sierra Madre, Carpathian, Transantarctic, Karakoram, Caucasus, Sudirman, Hindu Kush, Ural, Pyrenees

   Yes, indeed, mountains cover a quarter of Earth's land surface.

   Such vast and wild space, yet home to 12% of our human family.

c. Have you approached a mountain range across the valley and been awestruck by its majesty? Have you been up on a peak where the oxygen is thin? Seen the extraordinary vista above the treeline?

   Have you camped up where it feels you can almost touch the Milky Way? Have you known the need to string up your food out of bear's reach (for this is her territory even more than your own)?

   Have you felt the rocky ground beneath you on a mountain trail, listened to the varied song of the wind on a bluff, smelled the boreal forest, heard the rush of a waterfall?

d. Mountains were significant to our biblical ancestors as well. The Bible has 363 references to mountain or mountains. That is nearly one for every day of the year. An example: Moses' final blessing of Joseph:
   "Blessed by the Lord be his land... with the finest produce of the ancient mountains,
   and the abundance of the everlasting hills."
   (Deuteronomy 33:13, 15)

   Elijah meets God on Mt. Horeb, in the stunning silence that follows the wind, earthquake and fire. (1 Kings 19:11-13)

   At least 33 mountains are named explicitly: Mount Sinai, Mount Carmel, Mount Zion, Mount Tabor, Mount Samaria, Mount Moria, Mount Ephraim, Mount Zalmon – the litany goes on – and of course the Mount of Olives.

   Isaiah exhorts them: "Break forth into singing, O mountains." (Isaiah 44:23)

   And he gives us that beautiful passage read in the opening prayer: "How beautiful upon the mountains are the feet of the messenger who announces peace..." (Isaiah 52:7)

e. Almost a quarter of the world's forests (23%) are in her mountains.

   Their biodiversity is a marvel: 25% of the variety of life forms found on the land surface of Earth are in the mountains.

   With their ability to generate storms and contain snowpack and natural reservoirs, mountains provide more than half of humanity's fresh water.

   In the Book of Isaiah, God assures us of his enduring love: "For the mountains may depart and the hills be removed, but my steadfast love shall not depart from you" (Isaiah 54:10).

   It is much-needed assurance in these times when the glaciers are melting at a devastating rate; when the biodiversity of species in the mountains is threatened by pollution, encroaching human communities, and climate change; when the very storm patterns formed by mountains, and vital to life in them – and us – are changing.

Exercise 2: "The very stones would cry out" (28–33 min.)

The purpose of this exercise is to acknowledge our grief, pain, fears, and sorrows for the world and consciously allow God into it or to share it with God. If tears come, remember that they are a gift from and to God.

Introduction (to be read aloud or paraphrased) (3 min.)

Jerusalem sits at 2,600 feet (785 metres) above sea level, on a plateau in the Judaean Mountains between the Mediterranean and the Dead Sea. When Jesus made his final journey into Jerusalem on a donkey (Luke 19), the crowds hailed him with praise and palm branches. Jesus' closest friends marvelled at the scene. Jesus replied that even if the people had been silent, the very stones would cry out… those stones of the Judaean Mountains with which Jesus was so familiar.

Many Indigenous peoples consider stones to be story keepers. This resonates in Jesus' words as well. The mountains, the hills, the stones have existed for eons. They have witnessed all of human history. The Celts built grief cairns out of stones from the local landscape – a place to locate and express their grief.

The first Christmas of the Covid pandemic, when we were unable to gather in our churches to pray, Yvonne joined with a small church community for an outdoor service:

> The sun had set and it was gently snowing as we gathered at the river. The minister told of how he had found himself, throughout that first year of the pandemic, at a loss for words. "I have no words," he repeated again and again as he shared his story of the pandemic. He then passed around a basket of small stones. The stones hold our stories; they "speak" – as Jesus knew – when we cannot.

We are often at a loss for words when encountering deep grief or trauma. What would the stones cry out today about the ecological crisison Earth?

Prayer (25–30 min.)

Place the empty basket in the centre of the circle. Pass the basket of stones around the group and invite each person to take one.

Invite them to: Hold the stone in your palms; perhaps touch it against your forehead, your heart, your belly, your throat. Feel the stone's existence.

Imagine what the stone might "cry out" about the ecological crisis… about the Earth's and humankind's suffering and struggles… What grief, trauma, fear, or sorrow might it cry out about even if we are silent?

Pause, in silence for prayer, reflection, listening…

Invite the members, as they are ready, to place their stone in the basket in the centre of the circle, voicing anything they can or wish of what the stone would cry out or any sorrow or grief that they themselves want to say. Or, if they have no words, they may place their stone silently in the basket.

When the sharing is finished, close by singing or playing the Taizé chant "O Lord, Hear My Prayer."[73]

The stones continue as a locus for grief and pain. The basket of stones is meant to remain throughout the retreat program. Choose a place for it to reside between sessions – perhaps in the room where the group meets, or perhaps the group can designate a member to be the keeper of the stone basket and bring it back each week.

Or there may be a suitable space outside where the group wishes to place the stones more permanently. This can be done by the whole group or by one or more designated persons.

Break (10 min.)

Exercise 3: Claiming and Honouring Our Talents (25–30 min.)

Depending on the available time, this can be done in one full circle, like the previous exercise, or you can break out into smaller circles of five or six people.

Pass the asket of unused stones around, again inviting each person to take one.

Again, hold the stone in your hands. The stones hold the rest of our stories, too, not just our grief or pain. They hold the story of our abilities, our innate gifts, our skills, our accomplishments. Perhaps imagine Jesus sitting in front of you, his hands clasped around yours. Jesus, the Christ through whom all things are created. Son of the Living God who knows – as the Psalmist tells us – when we sit and when we lie down, who knitted us in our mothers' wombs. Christ who loves you unconditionally, without end. Let the stone and Jesus remind yo of your abilities in this challenging time on Earth. Whether they be problem-solving or simple kindnesses that make life gentler for others, all your skills and talents contribute to the kingdom of God that Jesus preached. Perhaps you will be shown some things you overlook or take for granted. Honour it all as best you can.

Play "Take, O Take Me as I Am"[74] (by John Bell).

Take 3 to 5 minutes, while gentle music or sounds of nature are played, to encourage silent, reflective prayer.

Invite people to share about their talents and abilities. This stone they keep and take home as a reminder of what they have claimed.

Closing Prayer (5 min.)

Reread the following passages from Isaiah:

> *How beautiful upon the mountains are the feet of the messenger who announces peace. (Isaiah 52:7)*
>
> *For the mountains may depart and the hills be removed,*
> *but my steadfast love shall not depart from you. (Isaiah 54:10)*

Play or, better yet, sing together the hymn "For the Beauty of the Earth."[75]

Continuing Your Prayer at Home

* If you are or have been blessed by time in the mountains, take time to recall those moments, one at a time. Recall what you did, what creatures you encountered, how you felt, how it affected you… Savour it. Let it bless you again. Perhaps journal about them; write an ode to the mountains; or draw them, make a collage, or work with clay to express something of your experience.
* If nothing else, we can be conscious of our relationship with mountains through our water. When you turn on a tap, thank the water and the mountains that are such a vital water source.
* View the movie *The Eagle Huntress* or another film that highlights the life of mountains.
* As always, take time to quietly read the opening reflection for the next session. Read it through slowly and attentively. At the end of your reading, let what you have read sift through your mind. What do you still hold as a thought, an emotion, a reaction? What struck you in your reading. What moved you? Note what is stirring in your heart. Jot down some of your thoughts as you prepare for the next session.

Session 4

Forest

Opening Reflection

John McCarthy, SJ

Let us mention, for example, those richly biodiverse lungs of our planet which are the Amazon and the Congo basins, or the great aquifers and glaciers. We know how important these are for the entire earth and for the future of humanity. (*Laudato Si'*, #38)

The beloved Amazon region stands before the world in all its splendour, its drama and its mystery. God granted us the grace of focusing on that region .... (*Querida Amazonia*, #1)

The River (Amazon Forest) (iStock / JohnnyLye)

I was seduced at an early age – tempted by rock, wind, and water, enticed by the open heathlands and dense forests, infatuated by nature and wildness. Mesmerized, obsessed, blinded, I fell for nature – the affair continues.

Born in St. John's, Newfoundland, on the far eastern edge of North America, near the confluence of the cold Labrador Current and the warm Gulf Stream, I was formed by the rhythm of the North Atlantic, by the ebb and flow f tide and wave, fog banks and migrating whales, screeching gulls and briny, mesmerizing winds. But it was to the interior of the island that I was drawn – to that often fog-strewn mosaic of forest, bog, and barren that stretched to the horizon and beyond. It was there that I seemed to be most at home. Many a day was spent tramping aross these sylvan wilds with family and friends, trout fishing, berry picking – or, as was often the case, simply alone in solitude, embraced by peace and beauty. The boreal forests of Newfoundland became my nursemaids, my companions, my gods. The forests spoke of mystery, of love, of divine silence.

Tucked between the Arctic tundra to the north and the temperate forests and grasslands to the south, the northern forest acts as a circumpolar halo of green and blue – the great boreal biome. Named after Boreas, the Greek god of the north wind, also known by its Russian name, *taiga*, the boreal region holds about 30% of the world's forests.[76] The coniferous pine, spruce, larch, and fir mix with the deciduous birch, aspen, and poplar to create one of the great forest regions of the world. Given its relative remoteness and low population density, the boreal region boasts an ecological integrity with abundant wildlife, intact ecosystems, and unparalleled freshwater sources.[77]

We did not create the forest – or anything of nature, for that matter. We can and do change forests, use forests, tend forests, care for and love forests, manipulate forests, destroy forests, but we can never create a forest. We may plant a forest that with time may not look too much different from a naturally regenerated forest. But we cannot create the internal dynamics of forests or the life histories of all the species that make up a forest. We cannot manufacture the inherent rules and probabilities that define the totality of what we call a forest. No amount of intellectual, scientific, or economic sophistication can create or re-create the forest. Forests, as are all other things of nature, are created, not made. By that very fact, forests possess an intrinsic integrity, an integrity that does not depend on their actual or potential utility for humans.

The forest simply is. And therein lies its beauty and meaning. Into its arms you fall. Before its gaze you stand in awe. Within its silence you rest. Once, while on my annual eight-day retreat, I discovered a secluded grove of majestic red and silver maple hidden from the open fields and the well-trod path. During those days of prayer and silence, the grove became my chapel, my cathedral. Each day, it drew me beyond the retreat house, down the worn path, away from the field, into myself, into something of God. And there I sat, my back propped up by a hardened trunk, knees bent, feet firmly planted on a moss-covered log lying upon the rich, leaf-layered forest floor.

The forest grove became for me a sacred grove. Sacred as it spoke to me of life and spirit that fed my soul. My guard lessened. My heart awakened. I was able to wait, to listen, to rest, to take root in the moment, embraced by the solitude of the forest. A complexity of green, ordered to life and continuity, the forest enacted no toll, no price. For me it spoke something of the Divine. Was not this created grove a mirror, an image, of its Creator? Within the midst of the forest, something, someone spoke to me in ways ineffable. Come with me into the forest. And there I will speak to your heart.

In the forest, death is never the final word. From death comes the possibility of new life. The death of trees or stands provides growing space for new life. Seeds drop, twirl, and flutter to earth. Those seeds that survive and find a receptive home will germinate, take root, and reach for the light. Old logs on the forest floor, suitably decayed and moist, are a favourite germination site. The legacies of death function as nurse logs for the future. Sometimes, the regeneration is already present in the shade of the parents. It lies in a suppressed state, hanging on, until one day the canopy of mature trees is destroyed, and the small seedlings respond with vigour to the newfound abundance of soil nutrients and light.

Can we talk of the wisdom of the forest? Does it teach us something? Does the forest, in its myriad of manifestations, teach those with ears to hear and eyes to see? I have visited many kinds of forests – the cold boreal forests of northern Ontario and Labrador, the saline mangrove forests of coastal Philippines, the well-managed beech-spruce forests of the Belgian Ardennes, the high-altitude, old-growth subalpine forests of British Columbia, or the industrial pine plantations of the coastal plain of the southeastern United States.

Each forest has a story to tell, a history to remember, a lesson to be taught. I remember flying by helicopter low over the thick blanket of black spruce forests in Labrador, the "great land." Even if we had wished, there was no place to land. Mile after mile of green blanketed the earth, the result of past fires that raged across this landscape of spruce and caribou lichen. This contrasts with the managed French and German forests of the European heartland. To the untrained eye, a wild forest, but to the local foresters each tree is measured and known, with forest management plans centuries old.

Trees weather time. In all seasons, trees speak of splendour. Each season changes the texture and colour of the forest. In the fall, I trace my gaze across the field edge. The early spring flush of iridescent green, the weathered green of late summer, the mapled crimson, orange, and yellows of fall, the sombre greyness of winter. Each season speaks its own language.

The forest invites me to silence and security. The forest helps me to find my own voice, a voice that longs to bubble up through the conflicting layers and noise of my life. It does not judge or suggest but simply opens space and time to contemplation. The winds are muffled, the rain absorbed, the snowfall softened. To enter the forest is to enter the depth of stillness, the heart of solitude. For some reason, the still forest interior has always attuned my senses. I have felt right at home. My muscles relax, my pace slows, and my heart softens. Maybe that is why the monastic monks of old (and new) fled to the forests in search of sublime solitude: to mountain valley, watered valleys, or secluded forests to cleanse their souls and hearts.

I have tried to convey in this reflection my sense of the *sacredness* of the forest. Sacred in the sense that I personally cannot live without a relationship with forests. Sacred in the sense that forests are created out of Divine Love, hallowed, worthy of care and respect, consecrated to human dignity. Sacred in the sense that forests, like all creation, reveal something of the mystery and beauty of the Word of God.

Moose River, Hudson Bay Lowlands, Canada (John McCarthy, SJ)

Old-growth fir-spruce forests, northwest Newfoundland, Canada (John McCarthy, SJ)

Session 4: Forest

Preparation

* Select scents of fragrant forest trees such as pine, spruce, fir, etc. and/or branches of fragrant trees for participants to "smell" forest (4 or 5 is enough).
* Select varied tree branches, preferably some with leaves, some with needles (pine, fir, etc.), and with varied bark; roots are good, too, if available, for participants to "touch" forest (again, 4 or 5 is enough).
* Place the fragrances and branches in or near the circle so they can easily be passed around the group.
* Set up audiovisual equipment for viewing the video *The Man Who Planted Trees* (available on YouTube).
* One for each participant: wooden shims or pieces of birch bark or paper about 10 cm long (large enough for writing a short message); pencils.
* If you have a place outdoors for a small campfire, prepare this ahead of time (but don't light it until Exercise 2). If there is a woodstove or fireplace in the room where you are gathering, you can use that. Have the usual safety precautions at hand.

Snowy mountain forests, north of Vancouver, British Columbia (John McCarthy, SJ)

* Optional: Set up an audio-recording and speaker system to play the closing prayer. A Google search of "Amanda Palmer reads when I am among the trees" offers a well-read recording of the poem.

Opening Prayer (3 min.)

Read the following passages in a round, with readers taking turns around the group. Each line of blessing in the reading from Daniel could be read by a new reader (and the refrain could be spoken by the group).

For you shall go out in joy
and be led back in peace;
the mountains and the hills before you
shall burst into song,
and all the trees of the field shall clap their hands. (Isaiah 55:12)

Sing, O heavens, for the Lord has done it;
shout, O depths of the earth;
break forth into singing, O mountains,
O forest and every tree in it!
For the Lord has redeemed Jacob
and will be glorified in Israel. (Isaiah 44:23)

Blessed are those who trust in the Lord,
whose trust is the Lord.
They shall be like a tree planted by water,
sending out its roots by the stream.
It shall not fear when heat comes,
and its leaves shall stay green;
in the year of drought it is not anxious,
and it does not cease to bear fruit.
(Jeremiah 17:7-8)

Let the field exult, and everything in it.
Then shall all the trees of the forest sing for joy. (Psalm 96:12)

57 Bless the Lord, all you works of the Lord;
sing praise to him and highly exalt him forever.
58 Bless the Lord, you heavens;
sing praise to him and highly exalt him forever.
59 Bless the Lord, you angels of the Lord;
sing praise to him and highly exalt him forever.
60 Bless the Lord, all you waters above the heavens;
sing praise to him and highly exalt him forever.
61 Bless the Lord, all you powers of the Lord;
sing praise to him and highly exalt him forever.
62 Bless the Lord, sun and moon;
sing praise to him and highly exalt him forever.
63 Bless the Lord, stars of heaven;
sing praise to him and highly exalt him forever.
64 Bless the Lord, all rain and dew;
sing praise to him and highly exalt him forever.
65 Bless the Lord, all you winds;
sing praise to him and highly exalt him forever.
66 Bless the Lord, fire and heat;
sing praise to him and highly exalt him forever.
67 Bless the Lord, winter cold and summer heat;
sing praise to him and highly exalt him forever.
68 Bless the Lord, dews and falling snow;
sing praise to him and highly exalt him forever.
69 Bless the Lord, ice and cold;
sing praise to him and highly exalt him forever.
70 Bless the Lord, frosts and snows;
sing praise to him and highly exalt him forever.
71 Bless the Lord, nights and days;
sing praise to him and highly exalt him forever.

72 Bless the Lord, light and darkness;
sing praise to him and highly exalt him forever.
73 Bless the Lord, lightnings and clouds;
sing praise to him and highly exalt him forever.
74 Let the earth bless the Lord;
let it sing praise to him and highly exalt him forever.
75 Bless the Lord, mountains and hills;
sing praise to him and highly exalt him forever.
76 Bless the Lord, all that grows in the ground;
sing praise to him and highly exalt him forever.
77 Bless the Lord, you springs;
sing praise to him and highly exalt him forever.
78 Bless the Lord, seas and rivers;
sing praise to him and highly exalt him forever.
79 Bless the Lord, you whales and all that swim in the waters;
sing praise to him and highly exalt him forever.
80 Bless the Lord, all birds of the air;
sing praise to him and highly exalt him forever.
81 Bless the Lord, all wild animals and cattle;
sing praise to him and highly exalt him forever.
82 Bless the Lord, all people on earth;
sing praise to him and highly exalt him forever. (Daniel 3:57-82)

Exercise 1: Senses of Forests

(30 min.)

In each section below, the facilitator will need to keep time and guide the group to each next step. This allows participants to simply attend to the prayers of the senses.

a. Forest Image

This is an exercise of visio divina: visual contemplation of the divine. Brief periods of silent contemplation are followed by brief sharing.

Invite each participant to select one of the following four images – whichever one attracts them.

Silently gaze on the image(s)… Notice what you see… Notice what you feel…

Taking turns around the circle, share briefly in the group, in just two or three sentences, what you see. Do not specify which image you are viewing.

Having heard from others, return to the same image and gaze silently again. Allow your gaze to be affected by the views the others shared.

Again, taking turns around the circle, share briefly what you see.

Have one more visit with the image.

Take turns around the circle again, but this time, share just a word or phrase to express your feeling.

Tom Thomson, *Autumn Foliage*, 1915 (public domain)

Albert Bierstadt, *Giant Redwoods of California*, 1874 (public domain)

Old yellow birch, Salmonier River valley, eastern Newfoundland, Canada (John McCarthy, SJ)

Balsam fir-feathermoss forests, western Newfoundland, Canada (John McCarthy, SJ)

b. Forest Fragrance

Read (or invite a participant to read) the following passage aloud.

> I somehow figured that the prophet Isaiah was a forester – or at least somone who loved trees.
>
> "I will put in the wilderness the cedar, the acacia, the myrtle, and the olive; I will set in the desert the cypress, the plane and the pine together, so that all may consider and understand, that the hand of the

> Lord has done this, the Holy One of Israel has created it." (Isaiah 41:19-20)
>
> When I heard this passage proclaimed, I rejoiced in the fragrance of God. These trees of which Isaiah spoke are fragrant trees. How often we associate different forests and tree species with various fragrances. I remember well filling my senses with the fragrance of pine needles warmed by dry, arid winds of interior British Columbia, or the earthy, pungent odours rising from the freshly drenched humic forest floor carpeting the northern boreal forests of Labrador, or the evocative, dizzying colognes emanating from a linden tree in full bloom in the Vosges forests of eastern France. This is the voice of God, ripe, fresh, volatile ... Let anyone with noses smell![78]

Pass the scents or fragrant tree branches around the circle, one at a time. When the first is about a third of the way around, you could begin the second, and so on.

Invite participants to remain silent through this exercise and to focus just on their sense of smell and take their time and breathe in the scent as deeply as they like – once, twice, even a third time before passing it on. Perhaps they wish to close their eyes as they smell the fragrance. As they breathe, they can notice the scent, notice what it elicits in them – perhaps a feeling, or a memory... Just notice....

Remain in silence as the last people finish with the last scent.

c. Forest Touch

Pass the tree branches around the circle, one at a time. When the first is about a third of the way around, you could begin the second, and so on.

Again, invite participants to be silent, to close their eyes, and focus just on the sense of touch. The branches can even be passed *gently* with eyes closed; this can enhance the sense of touch.

This time, have them take their time, feeling the branch, with their fingers and hands, maybe brushing it against their cheek. Don't be in haste to pass it on. Again, have them notice: how the branch – this part of the forest – feels... sharp, soft, rough, smooth... And notice what it elicits in them.

Sharing

Take a moment to reflect on the two experiences of smell and touch. (You've already shared about the visual contemplation.) What moved you most? What do you want to take away with you? Consider what you would like to share briefly in the group.

Share, going around the circle.

Forest cutover, western Newfoundland, Canada (John McCarthy, SJ)

Exercise 2: The Forest Falls (20 min.)

Distribute the pencils and shims, bark, or paper.

Read the following passage aloud. As you listen, consider: What touches you or moves you? What captures your concern? ... your sorrow? ... your fear? ... your sense of loss?

We are living in probably the greatest period of human-caused deforestation on the planet. Deforestation is not expected to subside greatly in the near future. Increased pressure on the globe's forests will continue. More importantly, population and economic development pressures will increase

Forest cutover, near Deer Lake western Newfoundland, Canada (John McCarthy, SJ)

in the tropical forests of Asia, Africa, and South America, the last vestiges of the world's primary tropical forests. And even the great green halo of the world's boreal forests that covers the northern circumpolar mantle of the earth are beginning to feel unrelenting human pressures.

We need wilderness forests – safe havens for wildness and freedom of life and process. We need wilderness forests to fulfill our human desire for preservation of forests and other ecosystems. To let some places simply be is essential to our humanity and is a value for human culture. Culture is humanized when it refuses to exercise in full the power it may possess. To preserve or set aside forestlands is to exercise a respectful distance, a contemplative distance from the other. This mutuality, this asceticism of love ermits the forest to live in its fullness and integrity.

I lament the loss of forest boundaries. What would it be like to live in a world of no boundaries, of no region "out there" beyond the city or town or village? I fear that I would have nowhere to go, neither on foot nor in my imagination. Loss of landscape: is it not also loss of inscape?

Robert Pogue Harrison, in his study of the cultural meaning of forests, considers the loss of boundaries in the current deforestation as a key to understanding the ecological lament. He explains:

> The global problem of deforestation provokes unlikely reactions of concern these days among city dwellers ... We call it the loss of nature, or the loss of wildlife habitat, or the loss of biodiversity, but underlying the ecological concern is perhaps a much deeper apprehension about the disappearance of boundaries, without which the human abode loses its grounding ... Without

> such outside domains, there is no inside in which to dwell.[79]

When I first began field research in the boreal forests of Newfoundland's Great Northern Peninsula, I knew the watershed as essentially without roads. Over the next five years, I watched as the forest industry opened up the boreal forest wilderness with roads, landings, and clearcuts. I remember, in particular, driving one of the newly constructed roads that was pushed across the virgin bogs and fens on to the next patch of commercial forest. Crushed rock, freshly blasted, graded out over the wetlands. Incongruency, disconnectedness. I entered a world that only days before had been inaccessible except by foot or helicopter. It had been like that for centuries, andnow I was driving in comfort across this path of intrusion. I felt a deep sense of loss, of nostalgia, of lament for what was. The boundaries had shifted, and I felt lost.

Take a few moments of silent reflection, and again consider: What touches you or moves you? What captures your concern? ... your sorrow? ... your fear? ... your sense of loss?

Your concerns and your feelings are prayers to share with God. Write them briefly on the wood shim, bark, or paper.

If you have a space for a fire inside or outside the gathering space, place the shims in the fire, one at a time, naming what you are giving to the fire – to God – for God's care, transformation, help...

If you do not have a fire, name in the group what you have written, then take it with you and find a place tonight or tomorrow to give it over to the Earth – and God: bury it, put it in a river... Or one member of the group can take them all and do so.

Close by singing together the Taizé chant "O Lord, Hear My Prayer"[80] five to eight times.

Break (10 min.)

Keep the forest scents and branches out during the break for those who want to revisit them.

Exercise 3: Visio Divina with Tree of Life (15 min.)

Jesus Christ was crucified on a tree: the Tree of Life. Rooted in earth, reaching out toward heaven, the Tree of Life binds heaven and earth, reconnecting the dualities of life. God, humanity, and all creation are linked across the span of the Tree. Body and soul, night and day, matter and spirit, male and female – all the couplings of life find unity in the crucified Tree of Life. Again and again, in creation and in Jesus' crucifixion and resurrection, from suffering and death springs forth new and abundant life.

Spend some quiet time with the images of the Tree of Life on the next page...

> What do you notice? What attracts you or disturbs you? How do you respond interiorly?
>
> Perhaps speak – in your imagination – with the Tree of the Cross, the Tree of Life. Speak from your heart...
>
> ...And listen. What can the Tree of Life – the Paschal Mystery – tell you of how to live today's ecological challenges? ... How you can live in the light of the suffering, death, and resurrection of Jesus Christ?
>
> When you have finished, write some notes in your journal to help you remember what happened for you ...; what you felt ...; what you saw, heard, understood...

View the Blake Debassige image *Tree of Life*, commissioned for the Anishinabe Spiritual Centre, Espanola, Ontario: https://artvalue.ca/artwork/Blake-Randolph-Debassige/Untitled-Tree-of-Life-Crucifix/91010108516883/

Image of the Cross in tree cross-section (John McCarthy, SJ)

Exercise 4: Film: *The Man Who Planted Trees* (50 min.)

1. View the film together (30 min.).

2. Spiritual conversation: Do this in groups of five to seven people. (20 min.)

Round #1: What resonates within you after praying with the Tree of Life and viewing *The Man Who Planted Trees*? Share one or two insights.

Round #2: What did you hear within the group during the first round? Any commonalities? Any differences?

Round #3: What do you take away with you from the film and from the rest of this session?

Closing Prayer (3 min.)

Read the Mary Oliver poem "When I Am Among the Trees" aloud, or play the recording (see the preparatory notes for this session). The poem is easily found online.

Continuing Your Prayer at Home

* This week, be attentive to the trees, woodlands, and forests around you. Take some time to appreciate them and to ponder what they may be telling you. What invitations do you sense? What strikes you? Jot a few notes in your journal. Give thanks for the beauty of trees and forests. Give thanks for the gift of trees and forests.

Ecclesia and the Crucified Christ, 1610. Hendrick Goltzius. Courtesy of The Cleveland Museum of Art

* As always, take time to quietly read the opening reflection for the next session. Read it through slowly and attentively. At the end of your reading, let what you have read sift through your mind. What do you still hold as a thought, an emotion, a reaction? What struck you in your reading? What moved you? Note what is stirring in your heart. Jot down some of your thoughts as you prepare for Session 5.

Yellow Birch crown, Salmonier River valley, eastern Newfoundland, Canada (John McCarthy, SJ)

Session 5

Desert

Opening Reflection

Trevor Scott, SJ

The Desert in Popular Imagination Today

Of all the ecological landscapes reflectedupon in this retreat, perhaps the most difficult, the most uninviting, are deserts. Most of us are not naturally drawn to them. In our popular imaginations, they are hot, dry, and empty. Yet, the desert has the power to draw people in… Abram, Moses, Elijah, Jesus, the ancient Greek historian Herodotus, the French writer Antoine de Saint-Exupéry, the English military commander T.E. Lawrence (Lawrence of Arabia), the British explorer Wilfred Thesiger, the Canadian novelist Michael Ondaatje, the American essayist Edward Abbey… and to a lesser degree, me.

In his autobiography, *The Life of My Choice*, Wilfred Thesiger writes of the allure and mark of the desert upon him:

> No man can live this life and emerge unchanged. He will carry, however faint, the imprint of the desert, the brand which marks the nomad; and he will have within him the yearning to return, weak or insistent according to his nature. For this cruel land can cast a spell which no temperate clime can match.[81]

In his desert refletions, *Desert Solitaire*, Edward Abbey captures his wonder of getting lost in the American desert of the southwest, completely alone in 33,000 acres of desert "emptiness":

> … the sole inhabitant, usufructuary, observer and custodian … I am here not only to evade for a while the clamor and filth and confusion of the cultural apparatus but also to confront, immediately and directly if it's possible, the bare bones of existence, the elemental and fundamental, the bedrock which sustains us. I want to be able to look at and into a juniper tree, a piece of quartz, a vulture, a spider, and see it as it is in itself, devoid of all humanly ascribed qualities, anti-Kantian, even the categories of scientific description. To meet God or Medusa face to face, even if it means risking everything human in myself. I dream of a hard and brutal mysticism in which the naked self merges with a nonhuman world and yet somehow survives still intact, individual, separate. Paradox and bedrock.[82]

When I was a Jesuit novice beginning my spiritual formation, my Jesuit brothers and I were asked to undertake a month-long pilgrimage to help us deepen our faith in and dependency upon God's providence. With a one-way bus ticket and only $35 dollars in my pocket, I made my way from Saint Paul, Minnesota, to Santa Fe, New Mexico… I travelled to the desert of the American southwest to strive to meet God face to face, like the earliest of Christians. I was led to the Benedictine Monastery of Christ in the Desert, where I spent time praying upon my religious vocation and working for my lodging surrounded by the red-tinged Mesa desert cliffs. It was not a dramatic time, but it was a time that has resonated something deep within my faith since. It was my first time in a desert. Residing in the monastery, I was especially conscious of God within it in ways I might not have been otherwise. I also came to see that I was in the desert by choice. Whereas a woman I met there was not. It was her brother who drew her to the New Mexico desert every year… to Christ in the Desert Monastery in particular.

Her brother used to visit this holy ground within the desert every year. One year, while out hiking along the mesa cliff trails surrounding the monastery, he had a fatal fall. Every year since then, his sister travels to the desert to be near to her brother once again, to the memory of him. For her, the desert has become an annual pilgrimage of needed spiritual connection.

Wilfred Thesiger wrote to his mother, "It is curious how the desert satisfies me and gives me peace … You cannot explain what you find there for those who don't feel it too, for most people it is just a howling wilderness."

There is no single image of deserts nor any single attitude toward them. They are both attractive and unappealing, inviting and forbidding, depending upon who you talk to. They can be seen either as a fruitful wilderness or a barren wasteland, as a damned or a sacred place.

In our popular imagination, the deserts of our world are places of lifelessness. But in the imaginations of our monotheistic religious traditions, such as Christianity, regeneration of life is possible in the desert… especially in the desert.

The imaginations of artists can help us more deeply appreciate this process of life, death, and resurrection that the empty capacity of the desert allows to take place. The contemporary German artist Anselm Kiefer believed art had the inherent capacity – even the responsibility – to reflect and respond to our religious and spiritual insights.

While a student at the University of Freiburg, Kiefer spent holiday time at the Dominican monastery of La Tourette, designed by Le Corbusier, one of the most influential modern architects of the 20th century. The monastery was pioneering in its design and use of building materials. It was one of the earliest buildings primarily constructed of giant slabs ofgrey concrete that were meant to give the impression of a building in ruins. This style of building is common today, though not many find it appealing.

View a photograph of architect Le Corbusier's Sainte Marie de la Tourette in France.
(Google keyword search: 'Sainte Marie de la Tourette' 'Corbusier')

La Tourette, as a building, was no ordinary monastery for Kiefer in which to ponder himself and his relationship with God. For the artist, the ruin-like, even desert-like building of La Tourette was a source of immense spiritual and creative inspiration.

> [La Tourette] was an inspiring building in the sense that a very simple material, a modern material, could be used to create a spiritual space. Great religions and great buildings are part of the sediment of time; like pieces of sand. Le Corbusier used the sand to construct a spiritual space. I discovered the spirituality of concrete – using earth to mold a symbol, a symbol of the imaginative and he spiritual world.[83]

View the church in the monastery designed by Le Corbusier.
(Google keyword search: 'Sainte Marie de la Tourette church' 'Corbusier')

The deserts in our world are perhaps the most difficult ecosystems in our world to appreciate, similar to the difficult appeal of concrete modern churches today for so many. Deserts are considered the wastelands of our world, with so little evident life. Though their beauty may not appeal to us in any conventional way, they do hold great aesthetic and spiritual power… potentially. Anselm Kiefer strives to embody this desert-like appeal and power in his own art.

> My aim isn't to create an artwork that's as interesting as possible. Or even beautiful. I don't want anything that's superficially beautiful … My work should come off totally unimpressively … It's not the brilliant, but rather the banal things that contain those elements that carry us farther … the banal is the best starting point for one's own discoveries.[84]

View the Anselm Kiefer painting *The Orders of the Night, 1996.*
(Google keyword search: 'Anselm Kiefer' 'Orders of the Night, 1996')

Like the banality of exposed concrete churches that we are all familiar with, and that so many do not find spiritually inspiring in any conventional way, the banality of the baked or frozen sands and soil of the desert does hold the power of our agency toward deeper relationship with our God in ways we could never have imagined.

Session 5: Desert

Preparation

* Several containers of fine sand.

Opening Prayer (2 min.)

Allured into the desert,
With God alone, apart,
There spirit meets spirit,
There speaks heart to heart.
Far, far on that untrodden shore,
God's secret place I find;
Alone I pass the golden door,
The dearest left behind.

There God and I—no other;
Far from other men and women.
Or rather, amidst the crowd and tumult,
Still, Lord, alone with You.
Still folded close upon Your breast,
In field, market, or street,
Untroubled in this perfect rest,
This isolation sweet.
O God, You are far other
Than men and women have dreamed and taught,
Unspoken in all language,
Unpictured in all thought.
You God are God—we only learn

What this great Name must be,
Whose raptured heart within us burns,
Because we walk with You.
Stilled by Your wondrous Presence,
This tenderest embrace,
The years of longing over,
Do we behold Your Face;
We seek no more than You have given,
We ask no vision fair,
Your precious Blood has opened Heaven,
Where we have found You there.

O weary souls, draw near Him;
To you I can but bring
One drop of that great ocean,
One blossom of that spring;
Sealed with His kiss, my lips are dumb,
My soul with awe is still:
Let him that is thirsty but come,
And freely drink his fill.

—*Gerhard Tersteegen (1697–1769)*

Exercise 1: The Deserts of Our World (20 min.)

Quietly read through and reflect upon the following characteristics of deserts.

Alternatively, as a large group, take turns reading through these characteristics, with one person each reading aloud each section of characteristics for the group.

Global deserts (Brokyr8, CC BY 4.0 <https://creativecommons.org/licenses/by/4.0>, via Wikimedia Commons)

Overview of Our World's Deserts

- Deserts cover around one-fifth of our Earth's surface on every continent.
- They are home to nearly one billion people.
- In our popular imaginations, we often think of deserts as hot, dry, empty seas of shifting sand dunes.

- Though many deserts are quite hot, with temperatures as high as 54°C (130°F), many deserts are very cold… the Arctic and Antarctic deserts in particular.
- Most deserts, far from being empty and lifeless, are filled with plant, animal, and organic life.
- Many deserts are made up of shifting sands, which we are all imaginatively familiar with, but also of mountains, ridges, rock, ice, and even salt flats.
- What is common among deserts is their dryness.
- Deserts contain little water for organic life… or lots of frozen water.

Kinds of Deserts

There are four general types of deserts on our planet:

- **Subtropical deserts**
  - ⁎ Sahara Desert, in northern Africa (the world's largest desert)
  - ⁎ Kalahari Desert, in Southern Africa
  - ⁎ Tanami Desert, in northern Australia
- **Coastal deserts**
  - ⁎ Atacama Desert, on the Pacific shores of Chile
  - ⁎ Namib Desert, on the Atlantic shore of southwestern Africa
- **Rain shadow / Interior deserts**
  - ⁎ Mojave Desert, in the shadow of the Sierra Nevada Mountains of the western United States
  - ⁎ Gobi Desert, in China and Mongolia bordered by the Himalayas mountain range
- **Polar deserts**
  - ⁎ Arctic Archipelago, at the top of our world
  - ⁎ Antarctica, at the bottom of our world

Water in the Desert

- ⁎ Rain is the main source of water in a desert… but very scarce, and therefore precious!
- ⁎ Groundwater – the accumulation of rainwater over prolonged periods of time – is another main and more dependable source.
- ⁎ Desert dwellers rely on groundwater stored within natural aquifers below the surface, where it can remain for thousands of years.
- ⁎ This underground water can rise to the surface through springs or seeps, creating fertile green oases.
- ⁎ People, animals, and plants surround these oases as stable sources of not only water but also food and shady shelter.

Engineering for Water

- ⁎ Not all groundwater springs to the surface.
- ⁎ Many desert cities depend on underground water accessed through drilling, such as in the American Southwest and the Middle East.
- ⁎ Drilled aquifers come with environmental costs. Drilling into underground water easily overtakes the aquifer's volume and rate of rehabilitation, leading to water shortages and related environmental catastrophes.
- ⁎ The Mojave Desert is sinking due to aquifer depletion. The growing desert community of Las Vegas is using water faster than the aquifer is being refilled.
- ⁎ The engineering of rivers to help distribute and store water in a desert also takes place.
- ⁎ The Nile River along the eastern edge of the Sahara Desert provides the most reliable and

abundant source of fresh water in northeastern Africa.

* Between 1958 and 1971, Egypt constructed the massive Aswan Dam on the Upper Nile near its border with Sudan for its hydroelectricity and freshwater needs.
* Through the creation of Lake Nasser along the dam, Egypt was able to store fresh water for its communities' and agricultural needs against times of drought.
* But such freshwater preservation projects can easily lead to the creation of multi-state tensions.
* When deserts and water supplies cross civil borders, conflicts over water rights ensue, such as with Egypt and Sudan, and among the states of California, Nevada, and Arizona within the Colorado River Basin with their rapidly growing populations.

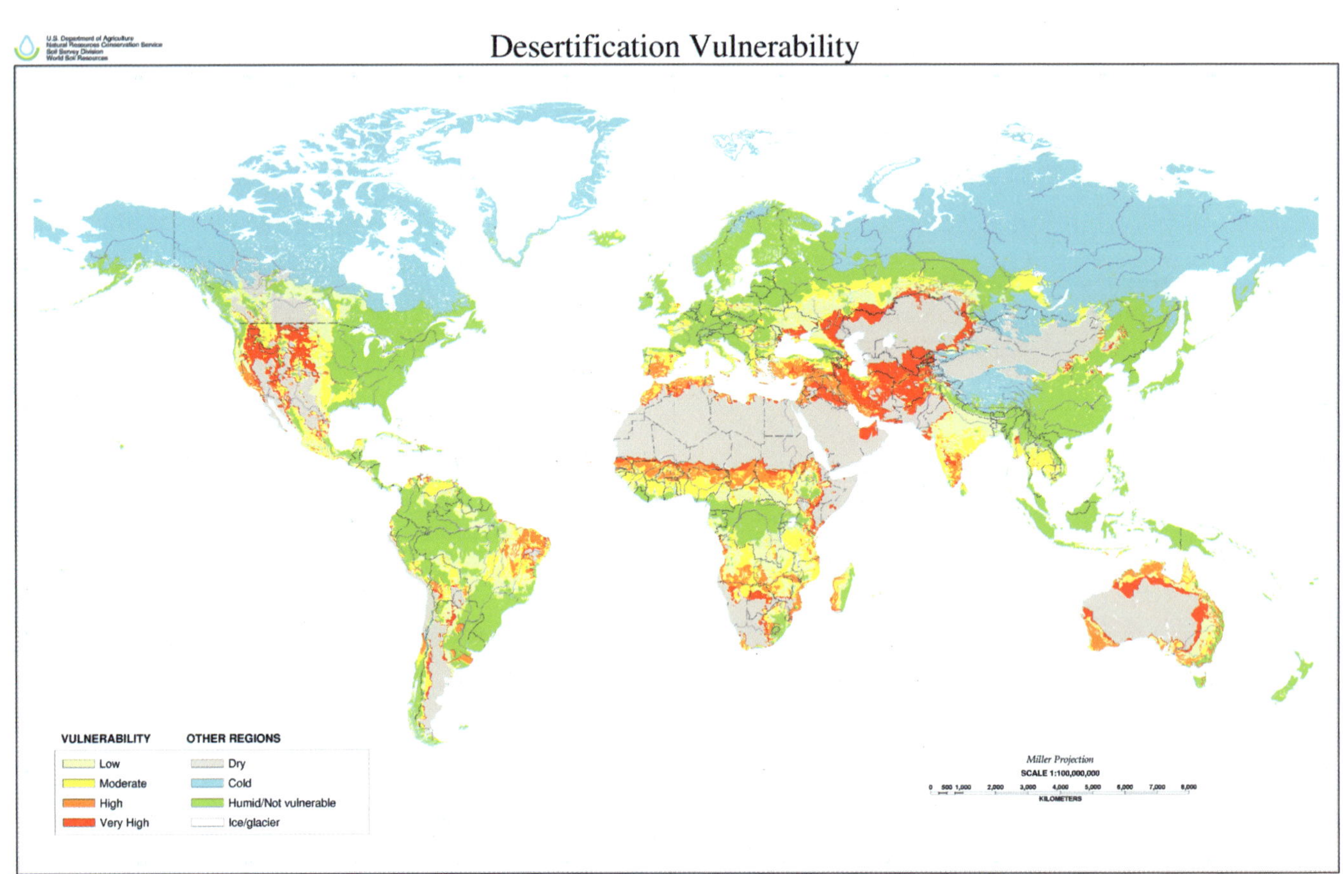

Desertification vulnerability (USDA employee, Public domain, via Wikimedia Commons)

Desertification

* Many of the deserts of our world today were not always so dry.
* Thousands of years ago, the Sahara Desert was considered much milder and moister.
* Climatologists consider this time as the "Green Sahara."
* Fossils and artifacts have given evidence that lime and olive trees, oaks, and oleanders once bloomed in the Sahara.
* Elephants, gazelles, rhinos, giraffes, and people used stream-fed pools and lakes.
* This un-desert-like environment existed as recently as 25,000 years ago.

* Desertification is the process of land transformation through which productive croplands gradually become non-productive, desert-like environments.

* The primary cause of desertification is human overactivity – the overuse of natural resources for short-term gain at the expense of long-term sustainability.

* Examples of overuse are the overgrazing of livestock, cutting down of forests, overcultivation of farmland, and poor irrigation practices.

* Overgrazing and deforestation remove the vegetation that anchors the soil, allowing the winds and flowing waters to easily erode the nutrient-rich topsoil.

* Hooves from grazing livestock compress the soil to the degree that it can no longer absorb water and fertilizers.

* The most vulnerable places in our world susceptible to desertification include the following:

    - Patagonia (in lower South America)
    - Madagascar (along the eastern African coast)
    - Lake Chad (on the edge of the Sahara Desert)
    - The Great Plains of North America

Resources of the Desert

* Deserts are home to a significant percentage of our world's population.

* Their survival and cultural thriving rely on centuries of developed customs unique to the harsh conditions of the desert, from the nomads of the Sahara to the Inuit of the Arctic.

* The basic need to search for food and water has made nomads of the peoples of desert civilizations.

* Desert dwellers could be seen as treasure hunters in their quest of desert resources for survival, leading to uniquely rich cultural characteristics.

* Dependence upon animals, like camels and goats in more southern deserts, and caribou and walrus in more northern ones, has been a daily occupation for the peoples of these environments.

* In subtropical deserts, a variety of desert vegetation is found in oases and along the shores of rivers and lakes, such as the figs, olives, and oranges that have thrived in desert oases and been harvested for centuries.

* Deserts also hold economically valuable resources, such as oil reserves and precious metals.

* The desert resource we all know of – and even depend upon wherever we live in the world – is the massive oil reserves beneath the Arabian Desert of the Middle East.

* More than half of the discovered oil reserves of the world lie beneath the Arabian Desert.

Conclusion

* We have seen that deserts are often hostile places to avoid if we can.

* But the extremity of these environments also holds an imaginative fascination for us.

* We are imaginatively held by their potential power, dominance, and vastness.

* We work to preserve and tap into their imaginative and material resources. At the same time, we dread their growth.

(2 minutes of silent reflection)

Exercise 2: Group Reflection

(10 min.)

Reflect on the following questions as a group:

1. Through these physical descriptions of the various deserts, what is your overall impression of deserts?

   Do they enhance the well-being of our world? Are they destructive places in our world?

   Would you like to visit, or even live in a desert? Why or why not?

2. Have you ever visited a desert environment?

   Reflect upon your remembrance. How would you describe it to others?

   What did you find there? How did it affect you?

Exercise 3: Impressions of Sand

(20 min.)

1. **Contemplate this desert image of Israel in silence.** (5 min.)

Timna Park in South Israel (Bakusova / Dreamstime.com)

2. **Group sharing and activity** (15 min.)

- What struck you most about this desert environment in Israel from this image?
- Do you find the life shown in this desert image surprising or inviting? How?

Place some containers of sand around the room.

Though we feel dry and empty sometimes, we are filled with faith and life. Our lives affect the lives of those around us. As we interact with those around us, we make marks upon them. We impact those around us, often in small ways, sometimes in large ways. Sometimes for good, sometimes not. Sometimes as witnesses to God, sometimes not.

Spend a moment making impressions in the sand. As you press the sand, notice how you leave your mark. As you move through your life, you are leaving your mark on the people around you. As you make impressions in the sand, ask God to mould your life so that it gives a Christ-like witness to those around you and gives life to those around you.

Break (10 min.)

Exercise 4: The Desert Test

(22 min.)

Take turns reading aloud this modern retelling of Scripture (from *The Message* Bible) in the large group. (2 min.)

The Test

1-3 Next Jesus was taken into the wild by the Spirit for the Test. The Devil was ready to give it. Jesus prepared for the Test by fasting forty days and forty nights. That left him, of course, in a state of extreme hunger, which the Devil took advantage of in the first test: "Since you are God's Son, speak the word that will turn these stones into loaves of bread."

4 Jesus answered by quoting Deuteronomy: "It takes more than bread to stay alive. It takes a steady stream of words from God's mouth."

5-6 For the secod test the Devil took him to the Holy City. He sat him on top of the Temple and said, "Since you are God's Son, jump." The Devil goaded him by quoting Psalm 91: "He has placed you in the care of angels. They will catch you so that you won't so much as stub your toe on a stone."

7 Jesus countered with another citation from Deuteronomy: "Don't you dare test the Lord your God."

8-9 For the third test, the Devil took him to the peak of a huge mountain. He gestured expansively, pointing out all the earth's kingdoms, how glorious they all were. Then he said, "They're yours—lock, stock, and barrel. Just go down on your knees and worship me, and they're yours."

10 Jesus' refusal was curt: "Beat it, Satan!" He backed his rebuke with a third quotation from Deuteronomy: "Worship the Lord your God, and only him. Serve him with absolute single-heartedness."

11 The Test was over. The Devil left. And in his place, angels! Angels came and took care of Jesus' needs. (Matthew 4:1-11)[85]

Personal Activity: Alone in the Desert (20 min.)

1. Silently find a desert-like environment near you, indoors or outdoors, to spend time in for 20 minutes. Try to find an outwardly unappealing, uninspiring, seemingly empty space that would not initially seem to be a place of encounter with God (an empty ugly room, a laneway, a construction site, a polluted street, etc.).
2. In your chosen desert, read again the above encounter of Jesus in the desert, now in a more *lectio divina* style. Considering Jesus' experience in the desert with the wayward spirit:

* Ponder how the guiding Holy Spirit is present with you in this seemingly empty space, as the Angel was present with Jesus.
* How do you experience the Holy Spirit in this desert space?
* Discern and experience with gratitude this personal encounter with the Holy Spirit.
* How has this desert experience helped you better appreciate the importance of desertscapes for our relationship with God?

Exercise 5: The Biblical Desert

(10 min.)

Take turns reading the following passages aloud in the large group.

Desert Spirituality

The desert – or the wilderness – of the Middle East is the land of Scripture: of the Hebrew Bible, the Gospels, and the Qur'an. The desert is the backdrop of our encounter with God, beginning with the early peoples of Israel. It could even be said that the early Israelites were desert – wilderness – peoples. It formed them. It was through the desert, their experiences of the desert itself, that their identity was formed. It was through the desert that they came to settle in Israel, the Promised Land. These wilderness years for the Jewish peoples, like all formative years in each of our lives in many ways, was a time to both celebrate and lament. These years symbolized physical and mental hardship, sense of dislocation and dispossession, and trust and doubt in God's sustaining presence.

The Wilderness as Absence

Though the early Israelites were successfully led through the desert into the land of Israel and nationhood, as promised by God, this exodus is remembered also as a time of bitterness, complaint, unfaithfulness, and sometimes rebellion. The wilderness experience of the desert was among the lowest points in the history of the formation of Israel. Later biblical writers used it as a warning of what should not happen again through repeated unfaithfulness.

The writers of the Pentateuch did not celebrate the desert experience. They warned the people of Israel to avoid repeating it. Their time in the desert was a time of passage to the Promised Land but also a lesson. In the Pentateuch, the desert is in many ways a negative place, a place of shameful memory of what took place there through little faith and disobedience.

The Wilderness as Ideal

The Pentateuch also shows the desert – the wilderness – as a place where God provides when it's needed most. The Jewish people, through Moses, were in continual communication with God, who did lead them successfully through it to the formation of their homeland, Israel. Though the desert was the place of Israel's faithlessness and rebelliousness, it was also the place of God's covenantal fidelity and providence amid the wilderness, providing Israel with manna from heaven and water from the rock cracked by Moses' staff.

In Genesis, Hagar flees to the desert in great distress over how she is mistreated by Abram's wife, Sarai. God comes to her in the desert to reassuringly call her back to Abram to bear his son Ishmael.

> The angel of the Lord found her by a spring of water in the wilderness, the spring on the way to Shur. And he said, "Hagar, slave of Sarai, where have you come from and where are you going?" She said, "I am running away from my mistress Sarai." The angel of the Lord said to her, "Return to your mistress, and submit to her." (Genesis 16:7-9)

After Hagar's son Ishmael and Sarah's son Isaac are born, Sarah wants Hagar banished. Upon reassurances from the angel of God, Abraham sends Hagar and their son Ishmael into the desert with a little food and water to eventually be provided for and elevated by the angel of God.

> So Abraham rose early in the morning and took bread and a skin of water, and gave it to Hagar, putting it on her shoulder, along with the child, and sent her away. And she departed, and wandered about in the wilderness of Beer-sheba.
>
> When the water in the skin was gone, she cast the child under one of the bushes. Then she went and sat down opposite him a good way off, about the distance of a bowshot, for she said, "Do not let me look on the death of the child." And as she sat opposite him, she lifted up her voice and wept. And God heard the voice of the boy, and the angel of God called to Hagar from heaven, and said to her, "What troubles you, Hagar? Do not be afraid; for God has heard the voice of the boy where he is. Come, lift up the boy and hold him fast with your hand, for I will make a great nation of him." Then God opened her eyes and she saw a well of water. She went, and filled the skin with water, and gave the boy a drink.
>
> God was with the boy, and he grew up; he lived in the wilderness, and became an expert with the bow. He lived in the wilderness of Paran; and his mother got a wife for him from the land of Egypt. (Genesis 21:14-21)

The outcome of Hagar's experience of escape and banishment into the desert is divine revelation. It was in the desert where God met her, provided for her, and entered into covenant with her through the future of her son. In Hagar's story we witness the wilderness not only as a place of banishment but also as a place of refuge and reassuring closeness with God.

These stories within the Pentateuch reveal that the desert is not only a negative space of absence and emptiness. It is also a place of God reaching out, God revealing God's self. It could even be said that this wilderness period within the early scriptural narratives was a time of great communicative intimacy between God's self and God's faithful.

It is this belief in the unique voice of God to be heard in the desert that gave birth to the monastic tradition of the early Christian church. Until Constantine converted to Christianity around 313, the Christian community existed only on the fringes of society. With Constantine's conversion, it became the official religion of the Roman Empire. With this official status, the gospel message was in turn gradually converted to fit into Rome's vision rather than the vision of Jesus and the early church.

With this growing perversion of the secularization of their faith, more and more followers of Christ fled the centres of the Roman Empire for the desert. Here in the deserts of Palestine, Egypt, and Syria, a new spirituality of the desert arose in response to an empire spirituality. These Christians were seeking a deepening of their relationship with Christ away from the interfering influence of the empire. In the desert they sought a deeper humility and silence rooted in a contemplative disposition and awareness.

As Jesus himself experienced going out into the desert as he began his public ministry, the desert continued to be seen as a place of spiritual testing and transformation, a place to ponder false dreams and visions of ourselves and to contend with our egos. Historically, at the time of Constantine's empire, it was the place to escape the energies of the empirical church, which were increasingly dominant and perverted with self-serving monarchical imagery and ideals.

The desire to enter the desert experience is to desire divestment of one's accumulated visions of oneself and one's ego. It is to want to know oneself and one's relationships with God intimately. It is also to behold the way the empire of the culture all around us has shaped our imagination, outlook, and values and to desire to expiate our enculturated self that has contaminated our understanding of and relationship with God through Christ.

The desert is also a place of vulnerability, where we seek to face and let go of our comforting knowledge of ourselves and God to meet a self and God we do not yet know nor could even imagine. Entering the desert can be seen as entering the spiritual furnace of our God to be transmuted more into God's own image from out of our false image of God.

But for many, this withdrawal from civic engagement to affectively ponder God's mystery more would have been seen as a retreat, an escape, from the responsibilities and difficult compromises demanded by society and disagreeable people. This is a continuing question that many today have related to those called to cloistered monastic life: Are they merely escaping from life's struggles? The fruits of their prayer and lives in the desert were soon witnessed, though. Within a few years, faith seekers looking for guidance and wisdom from these desert fathers were travelling to the desert to visit them – and, through them, God. They came to articulate the fruits of the depth of their relationship with God within the desert through pithy sayings and wise observations. These pilgrims following the desert fathers would even remain, forming desert communities and planting the seeds of the Christian monastic tradition.

Personal Contemplation and Group Sharing (20 min.)

Project upon a wall or screen for your group this image of Georgia O'Keeffe's *Red Hills and White Flower II*:

https://www.wikiart.org/en/georgia-o-keeffe/red-hills-and-white-flower-ii
(Google keyword search: 'Red Hills and White Flower II' 'Wikiart')

1. This image by the American artist Georgia O'Keeffe of a stylized blooming flower in the desert can be seen as a Christian metaphor of an emerging desert spirituality that we just read about. The image is located near Christ in the Desert monastery in New Mexico; O'Keeffe spent the last years of her life in that state. For 3 minutes, silently contemplate this image in light of the early history of the Christian faith emerging from the desert.

2. In your contemplation, ponder where you have personally discovered the life of your faith and spiritual sustenance in your own desert experiences. For 10 to 15 minutes, share with others in your group those life-emerging experiences.

Closing Prayer (2 min.)

A Prayer in the Desert[86]

The Wilderness and the Dry Land Shall Be Glad

Isaiah 35:1-10

1 *The wilderness and the dry land shall be glad,*
the desert shall rejoice and blossom;
like the crocus
2 *it shall blossom abundantly,*
and rejoice with joy and singing.
The glory of Lebanon shall be given to it,
the majesty of Carmel and Sharon.
They shall see the glory of the Lord,
the majesty of our God.
3 *Strengthen the weak hands,*
and make firm the feeble knees.
4 *Say to those who are of a fearful heart,*
"Be strong, do not fear!
Here is your God.
He will come with vengeance,
with terrible recompense.
He will come and save you."

5 *Then the eyes of the blind shall be opened,*
and the ears of the deaf unstopped;
6 *then the lame shall leap like a deer,*
and the tongue of the speechless sing for joy.
For waters shall break forth in the wilderness,
and streams in the desert;
7 *the burning sand shall become a pool,*
and the thirsty ground springs of water;
the haunt of jackals shall become a swamp,
the grass shall become reeds and rushes.
8 *A highway shall be there,*
and it shall be called the Holy Way;
the unclean shall not travel on it,
but it shall be for God's people;
no traveler, not even fools, shall go astray.
9 *No lion shall be there,*
nor shall any ravenous beast come up on it;
they shall not be found there,
but the redeemed shall walk there.
10 *And the ransomed of the Lord shall return,*
and come to Zion with singing;
everlasting joy shall be upon their heads;
they shall obtain joy and gladness,
and sorrow and sighing shall flee away.

Continuing Your Prayer at Home

* Visit a church whose architecture and interior design do not initially appeal to you.
* Spend time in this church, listening for the presence of God within it.
* Read orwatch nothing during this time. Just sit within it in silent listening.
* Remain prayerfully mindful of this desert-like environment.
* As always, take time to quietly read the opening reflection for the next session. Read it through slowly and attentively. At the end of your reading, let what you have read sift through your mind. What do you still hold as a thought, an emotion, a reaction? What struck you in your reading? What moved you? Note what is stirring in your heart. Jot down some of your thoughts as you prepare for Session 6.

Session 6

Prairie

Opening Reflection

Yvonne Prowse

The prairies. They're called pampas in South America, steppes in Eurasia, rangelands or savannah in Australia. I have had a lifelong dream to visit the African savannah, to see giraffes and elephants in their home with all the other beings of the savannah, including the extraordinarily tall grasses.

Depending on how you define them, grasslands make up 20 to 40% of our world's land area.[87] They can vary a great deal. Consider the frozen Arctic tundra and the hot African savannah. What do they all have in common? Grasses are the naturally dominant vegetation. Grasslands are defined by rainfall. Prairies and other grasslands are found where there's not enough regular rainfall to support the growth of forests, but not so little rainfall that a desert develops. Often it is mountains, such as the Rockies, that keep the rainfall at bay.

A dear friend of mine grew up on the Canadian prairies, and though she has lived in Ontario for decades, she still speaks of the prairies as home. They formed her. It is the landscape of her heart and psyche. She also loves Ontario, but every time someone talks about a long vista here, she points out that it cannot compare with the vast distances one sees in the prairies. She tells of walking home after dark on a December day with her sister, holding hands so they could take turns gazing on the *aurora borealis* while the other guided their footsteps.

As I write this, I sit with a piece of buffalo fur on my desk, a sacred gift from a friend when I was studying with a Native American Elder. It is a teardrop shape that just fits in the palm of my hand. Holding it, I can easily appreciate the warmth a robe of buffalo fur would have given the Plains Indians. The teaching and wisdom of the Indigenous peoples of the prairies is to use every part of the buffalo when they take her life. *All* life is sacred to them, and the buffalo especially so. Buffalo was essential for their survival on the plains in an earlier time, and they know they have a deep relationship with her. They wasted nothing. Even the snout had a special place in sacred ceremony.

Prairie dogs also captivate me. While buffalo can be taller than me, can weigh a tonne, could knock me over with a push of their head, and roam vast distances, a prairie dog is about a foot (30–40 cm) tall, lives in one small area, and burrows in the ground. Yet, these two natives of the prairies have some things in common. Both animals were slaughtered in such vast numbers in a short span of time, that they were on the brink of extinction. Both are also keystone species to the prairie ecosystem. They have such a pronounced effect on the biological diversity of the prairie system that without either of them, that ecosystem would be vastly different, and perhaps would not even exist.

As a spiritual director, I am fascinated with listeing, attentive listening… with hearing God in others and hearing God in many places – in the whisper of the wind moving across a field, in the call of the red-winged blackbird hailing the return of spring. I am intrigued with how we can listen to andfor God in our world. So, this story attracts me: When the United States Department of Agriculture, in 1920, developed a comprehensive plan for the eradication of prairie dogs from the great plains and deserts of the southwestern US, the Navajo Elders tried to stop them. They said, "If you kill all the prairie dogs, there will be no one to cry for the rain."[88] This may sound like a sentimental notion. But in fact, they were right. The government went ahead, and it devastated the whole ecosystem. Without the burrowing of the prairie dogs, which turns the soil, the soil suffered. Plants were lost. Insects and animals that feed on the plants died. The soil dried out and rain could not be absorbed. A virtual wasteland ensued.[89]

Actions such as that wholesale slaughter horrify me. But this Indigenous knowledge fascinates me and gives me hope. It reminds me of something Thomas Aquinas said: "A misunderstanding of nature will necessarily lead to a misunderstanding of God."[90]

It also has some affinity to a passage in the Book of Job:

> "Can you find out the deep things of God? Can you find out the limit of the Almighty?" … "But ask the animals and they will teach you; the birds of the air, and they will tell you; ask the plants of the earth, and they will teach you; and the fish of the sea will declare to you. Who among all these does not know that the hand of our God has done this? In God's hand is the life of every living thing and the breath of every human being." (Job 11:7, 12:7-10)

St. Paul writes in First Corinthians, chapter 12, of how we are all members of the body of Christ, and we cannot cut off a member and thrive. So, too, we cannot remove a species from our ecosystems and think it will have no ill efect. Nor can we kill off ecosystems in our world, as we are doing to the prairies, and think all shall be well. We are learning anew that all creation is part of the body of Christ.

Robin Wall Kimmerer, in her book *Braiding Sweetgrass*, emphasizes the reciprocal relationship we have with nature, whether we are aware of the relationship in that way or not. She points out that everything we do has a reciprocal consequence.

> In the western worldview we think of human people as outside of nature. And if we have a relationship with the living world it's altogether too often characterized as nothing more than consuming and in fact is a detrimental relationship. But the kind of reciprocity that I really try to invite readers into is the remembering that human people can be good for the land; that the ways that we interact with the land can in fact be very positive, so that in return for everything that we are given by the land, or everything that we take, we can give back.[91]

Kimmerer also talks of how we speak of other beings… be it sweetgrass or buffalo. When she began studying her native Potawatomi language, she realized that it is "impossible to say 'it'" about a bird or a butterfly or a maple tree. Rather, the Potawatomi language uses the same grammar of respect and relationship for our plant and animal relatives as humans do for one another.

Again, we can find corresponding wisdom in our Christian tradition: for example, St. Francis of Assisi's teaching, his way of calling the birds and the sun and moon "sister" and "brother," not "it." St. Hildegard of Bingen was a renowned herbalist and healer who knew the wisdom of plants intimately and preached about how all life is interconnected.

If we consider people's relationships with their pets, we see this is not a foreign idea. Rarely do people refer to their pet as "it." Many experience pets as members of the family. It deepened my relationship with nature, and with humans, too, when I began saying hello to beings on my walks in the woods, when I started calling them "you," as in "Oh, look at you, beautiful flower." Every time my cactus plant bursts into her showy blossoms, I tell her how beautiful she is and thank her for the life she brings into my home. I thank Grandfather Sun when I walk out of the house.

For better and for worse, the prairies are often thought of as the breadbaskets of the world. Wonderfully, they do indeed provide a vast percentage of our food. Sadly, it is at the expense of the natural prairie system, which is so rich and offers so much to us. I find help with this challenging dichotomy in another story my prairie friend shares, connecting it to Eucharist. As she was coming to know an Ontario woman who grew up in Italy, the two would share stories of their homelands. They had met through church, and as they shared about their native landscapes, they realized that one came from the land of wheat, the other from the land of wine; together, with their differences, they brought the gifts for Eucharist.

The earth gives us everything we need to live. Everything… food, clothing, shelter, warmth in winter. Our farmlands, much of which are in the prairies, remind us of this constantly. We can be reminded of this in Eucharist, too, when the priest says over the bread and wine, "fruit of the earth and work of human hands, it will become for us the brad of life… fruit of the vine and work of human hands, it will become our spiritual drink." In blessing our meals at home, we can also be reminded of this. Perhaps we can even begin to talk to the food and thank the brothers and sisters, as well as our Creator God, who gave their lives for us to live.

My soul turns into a tree,
And an animal, and a cloud bank.
... And asks me questions. What should I reply?

—From "Sometimes" by Hermann Hesse[92]

Session 6: Prairie

Preparation

* Set a table as a prayer focus with:
  - a sheaf of wheat or other prairie grass (if possible) – these could be dried, or perhaps a photo of a buffalo, pronghorn, etc.
  - bread in a basket or plate (or two, if the group is large) that can be passed around the group: the communion sharing will be non-sacramental, so the bread does not need to be unleavened; it would preferably be made by a local baker or someone in the group
  - a small pitcher of wine or grape juice (or two, as needed) to share, or fruit juice grown locally, such as from a local apple orchard
  - small cups for sharing the wine, as all will drink at the same time
* Hymn: "All Creatures of Our God and King"[93]

Opening Prayer (5 min.)

Read "The Canticle of the Sun," by St. Francis of Assisi:

The Canticle of the Sun

Most High, all-powerful, good Lord, Yours are the praises, the glory, the honor, and all blessings.

To You alone, Most High, do they belong, and no man is worthy to mention Your name.

Praised be You, my Lord, with all your creatures; especially Brother Sun, who is the day, and through whom You give us light.

And he is beautiful and radiant with great splendor, and bears a likeness to You, Most High One.

Praised be You, my Lord, through Sister Moon and the stars; in heaven You formed them clear and precious and beautiful.

Praised be You, my Lord, through Brother Wind, and through the air, cloudy and serene, nd every kind of weather through which You give sustenance to Your creatures.

Praised be You, my Lord, through Sister Water, which is very useful and humble and precious and chaste.

Praised be You, my Lord, through Brother Fire, through whom You light the night; and he is beautiful and playful and robust and strong.

Praised be You, my Lord, through Sister Mother Earth, who sustains us and governs us and who produces varied fruits with colored flowers and herbs.

Praised be You, my Lord, through those who give pardon for Your love, and bear infirmity and tribulation.

Blessed are those who endure in peace for by You, Most High, they shall be crowned.

Praised be You, my Lord, through our Sister Bodily Death,
from whom no living man can escape.

Woe to those who die in mortal sin. Blessed are those whom death will find in Your most holy will, for the second death shall do them no harm.

Praise and bless my Lord, and give Him thanks, and serve Him with great humility. Amen.[94]

Exercise 1: Large-group Sharing

(10 min.)

Pose the following question to the group:

* When you consider prairies, what images and/or firsthand experiences come to mind?

Allow a brief time for reflection, then invite sharing in the large group.

Exercise 2: Guided Meditation – A Virtual Journey to the Prairies

(45 min.)

a. **Introduction** (Can be read aloud by the facilitator or one of the participants)

The following meditation has two parts. In both, we allow God to use the imaginations God created in us to lead us closer to creation. First, a virtual journey, using our imaginations, into a natural prairie habitat. Second, a safe virtual encounter with one of God's other creatures.

St. Francis of Assisi is known for talking with the birds and the animals, speaking to "Brother Sun" and "Sister Moon." It is a practice that can teach us much and help usgrow closer to Mother Earth and to God. We can speak to other creatures, even landscapes and inanimate objects such as the moon, or a tree or glacier, as sisters and brothers. And we listen with the ears of our hearts and imaginations for what they can teach us.

This practice is not anthropomorphizing of other creatures. Rather, it allows us to meet another creature with reverence and appreciates that other creatures have knowledge – albeit differently than humans – and seeks to relate to them from within our humanity.

If you find yourself struggling to hear any message from the creature you encounter in the prayer, take another lead from St. Francis and try greeting him/her and praising the creature.

Joanna Macy, in her retreat work on reconnecting with Earth, suggests listening for two specific statements when you are encountering another creature in this way. Try employing these in your conversation, inviting the being to tell you:

"I am..."
"I want you to know..."[95]

As the facilitator reads the meditation, she or he will guide you in the practice and introduce the questions.

b. **Ask the group to gather into groups of three or four, forming a small circle.**

c. **The facilitator reads the following meditation.**

Sit in a relaxed yet attentive position,
And close your eyes if you are comfortable doing so.
Again, if you are comfortable doing so, take a deep breath in, and out...
... allowing yourself to grow quiet interiorly.

Imagine that you are in the prairies, in a place like Grasslands National Park in Saskatchewan, which features a natural prairie habitat and ecosystem.

In every direction, you can see vast distances. It is fairly flat with gentle rises, and as the grass waves in a soft breeze, it's akin to the gentle movement of water. Looking about you, you notice that there is a variety of grasses and plants. Maybe you can name some of the grasses, or maybe you just notice that some of the grass has a blue-green tone, and most is maybe 30 cm tall while others are a metre high. In places, you also notice wildflowers mixed in – daisies, goldenrod, violets, vetch, buttercups...

There are occasional trees – perhaps some aspen, and some buffalo berry with its sage green leaves and bright red berries. But mostly it is this mix of grass with wildflowers as far as the eye can see.

And some wildlife. Like the lizard that scoots by and the grasshoppers and butterflies flitting about the grass.

And what is that small prehistoric-looking little creature on the ground? His greyish flat, round body could fit in your two hands and makes him look like a cross between a baby armadillo and a lizard, except for those little spikes along his spine. Ah, so this is a horned toad. Hello, my friend.

You are aware that the prairie rattlesnake also makes her home here; perhaps you see one, thankfully at a distance. Her you give a wide berth.

And of course there are birds. Close your eyes and listen for a moment. How many different songbirds do you hear?

At a short distance is a group of bison. Far enough that they take no visible notice of you, but you can see their massive bulk, the amazing size of their heads; you can hear them browsing the grass. It gives you pause to consider just how much grass these herbivores need to consume each day.

American bison (Jack Dykinga, edited by Fir0002, Public domain, via Wikimedia Commons)

Over to the side is a prairie dog colony. If you stay quite still, they grow comfortable enough to come out of their holes and look about. Although they are classified in the squirrel family – and, indeed, their bodies are a bit similar to those of squirrels – you see that their heads are more like a miniature dog, except their ears look miniscule. As they stand up, you see their grey-white bellies against the tan fur. Can you also see their tails, with the black tips? This is what engendered their name: black-tailed prairie dog.

It is getting toward dusk now, and many other animals can be seen, as this is dinnertime. Off in one direction, perhaps you see some mule deer; beyond them are a few pronghorn: those majestic beings people often call antelope, though some think they look like small moose. They are unmistakable with those white stripes across their thick throats. You can tell which are the males by the longer horns that curl inward at the top.

The pronghorn suddenly bolt – not far, but they are definitely wary. You look about for what startled them. Ah, there is a coyote in the distance. A major predator for pronghorn, if she can catch one; but pronghorn are the fastest land mammal in the Western hemisphere, so coyote will have to be crafty.

Scanning the landscape down lower, in the grass, you spot a red fox, sleek and sly as can be.

What looks like a small owl with peculiarly long legs is hunting on the ground. Really, an owl hunting on the ground? This is the burrowing owl, which makes his home in burrows usually made by others, such as prairie dogs.

Now it is getting dark. Bats are starting to swoop along, hunting insects as they fly. You might realize that Bat has no interest in landing on you, and his echolocation lets him know how to keep far enough away. Perhaps you think bats are cool; or perhaps you are uneasy about them, as some people are. In this beautiful place, you breathe in acceptance that Bat is also God's creation and necessary to the true balance of this ecosystem.

Now in the dark, you stretch out on your camp recliner and gaze up at the night sky. Grasslands National Park is a designated Dark Sky Preserve, limiting light pollution at night. It is one of the largest and darkest in Canada. It is near the time of the new moon, so the stars will be more visible. You have been anticipating this rare opportunity to really see the Milky Way – that band of stars arcing across the whole sky – and maybe, if you're lucky, the aurora borealis.

You take in this beauty for a long while; [pause]... and then drift into a very peaceful dreamy state.

Now it is time to ask to be visited, gently, with grace and wisdom, by one of God's creatures – plant, animal, or other creation ...

Allow God to bring to mind the vista and all the creatures you encountered here, from the prairie soil to the stars, from the grass to the buffalo and butterflies. There is no rush. Appreciate them. Savour them.

(Pause briefly to allow images to come to mind.)

Gradually, or maybe rather quickly, one creature or being will stand out or seem to be calling to you or coming closer. It may be one you saw; it may be something new. Usually, a being sort of chooses us, rather than our choosing it. Be patient and as open-hearted as you are able, continuing to appreciate those that you have recalled... until one being emerges as seeking you out. See it with the eyes of your imagination. Welcome it... Greet it as brother or sister. Notice what you can about it... Offer a word of praise, to it or to God, and continue gazing on it with a gentle, appreciative, even loving gaze.

(Pause briefly)

Do not pepper this being with questions. Continue to be open and welcoming. If it allows your touch, and you are comfortable with that, caress it, or open your hand to hold it...

(Pause briefly)

Listen for what this being has to say and how they say it. Listen for them to complete the phrases that begin with:

"I am..." and "I want you to know..."

Take your time with this and respond to this being as you are moved.

(Pause a little longer)

Begin to draw your time with this being to a close, knowing you may always return to them. Is there anything else they wish to say?

Thank them. Wish them well.

When you are ready, bring your attention, silently, back to this room and the small circle of people with whom you are sitting.

Take another deep breath. Feel your feet on the floor.

d. Instructions for sharing:

One at a time, share within your small circle about your encounter. Each person will have 2 to 3 minutes to share (10 minutes total for the group). Tell the others who the creature was that met you and what they said about "I am" and "I want you to know." Also share anything you wish that was significant about the encounter that moved you.

(The facilitator can prompt the groups to change speakers every 2 to 3 minutes.)

Lastly, invite some sharing in the larger group. This time is not for everyone to share again about the encounter but to hear from a few in the large group about how the experience was for them. (5–10 minutes)

Break (10 min.)

During the break, return the chairs to one large circle.

> To live, we must daily break the body and shed the blood of Creation. When we do this knowingly, lovingly, skillfully, reverently, it is sacrament. When we do it ignorantly, greedily, clumsily, destructively, it is desecration. In such desecration we condemn ourselves to spiritual and moral loneliness, and others to want. – Wendell Berry[96]

Exercise 3: Non-Sacramental Communion Ritual[97] (30 min.)

Introduction (Have one or two participants read the text aloud to the group.)

The prairies are known as the breadbaskets of our societies. Even before agriculture, they were providing wild grains. Today, throughout the world, it is the prairies that provide most of our wheat. Thus, we associate them with the Bread of Life, with Eucharist.

And we see the reality of the life, death, and rebirth cycle always at play. We can get a felt sense of our dependence on Mother Earth for our food as well as everything else that sustains us. It is with this humbling awareness that we enter the eucharistic ceremony.

Pierre Teilhard [TAY-ard] de Chardin [shar-DAN] was a Jesuit priest and paleontologist born in Chardin, France, in 1881. He served as a stretcher bearer in World War I but is better known for his paleontology work on the steppes in China. In both places he found himself without the bread and wine he needed to celebrate Mass. In the trenches and on the steppes, he did not have an altar either.

This caused Teilhard to dive deep into the meaning of the Mass and to use a lot of imagery to find a suitable way to pray the Mass. Without bread and wine, but wanting to offer something back to God, he turned to the Universe – a universe that for 14 billion years has been, over the slow course of time, continually created and transformed. Simpler elements in the universe unite with others and become more than they are by themselves, such as when hydrogen and oxygen atoms bond to form water molecules. Or when yeast joins with flour and water to make bread.

Teilhard, opening his imagination, figuratively placed on his paten (the plate that holds the bread):

- *bees who go from flower to flower gathering nectar to make honey*
- *mothers who nurture their children in the womb*
- *scientists who spend years searching for cures or designing labour-saving devices*
- *all who strive each day to respond to the needs of a broken world*

When he considered the chalice, he placed in it:

- *the death he saw in the trenches of the war*
- *the destruction to his beautiful French countryside*
- *all that diminishes life*

Teilhard saw that God hungers for life; that Christ is present in all joys, in all that gives life – this is "bread." And Teilhard understood that God thirsts... thirsts to comfort all in the cosmos who suffer, who experience pain, exhaustion, anguish of death – this is the "wine" – the cup of suffering, the cup of salvation.

So, for Teilhard, to eat the bread is to truly relish the gifts of life, of creation. To drink the cup is to surrender, in trust, to God's constant care.

We do have bread and wine and will combine Teilhard's images with our participation in them.

Pass the bread around the circle, inviting each person to take a portion and hold it. Reflect on the joys, the blessings, of your day, your week, your life, and the life of the world. What do you want to name in the group?

(Facilitator invites sharing – in any order as individuals feel moved or taking turns around the circle.)

Once all have shared, the facilitator says:

We give thanks and savour God's goodness.
Take and eat.

Pass the wine and cups, again inviting participants to hold their portion. Gather the sorrows and suffering in your life, and the lives of your loved ones, your community, the world. What do you want to name in the group?

(Facilitator again invites sharing – in any order as individuals feel moved or taking turns around the circle.)

Once all have shared, the facilitator says:

We surrender, in trust, to God's loving care.
Take and drink.

Close by singing or listening to the hymn "All Creatures of Our God and King."

Continuing Your Prayer at Home

∗ Pray Grace at Meals

Take a moment of attentiveness at the start of each meal and pray a grace or blessing; perhaps at the end as well.

You might consider and thank the creatures (plant and animal) who gave their lives for your life, and all the beings – brother sun, sister rain… – as well as thanking God.

You might choose to write your own prayer. The writing would be its own form of attentiveness.

A few quotes for inspiration:

> We are speaking of an attitude of the heart, one which approaches lie with serene attentiveness, which is capable of being fully present to someone without thinking of what comes next, which accepts each moment as a gift from God to be lived to the full. ... One expression of this attitude is when we stop and give thanks to God before and after meals. (*Laudato Si'* #226–227)

> It has become clear to me that the concept of food itself is keyto the transformation of our ecological crisis. Unless our human species can open itself to the contemplation of food as a holy mystery through which we eat ourselves into existence, then the meaning of existence will contine to elude us. Our present cultural experience of food has degenerated into food as fuel, for supplying the energy for our insatiable search for that which will fill the hungers of the soul. When we understand that food is not a metaphor for spiritual nourishment, but is itself spiritual, then we eat food with a spiritual attitude and taste and are nourished by the Divine directly.
>
> Sr. Miriam Therese MacGillis[98]

> Eating with the fullest pleasure – pleasure that does not depend on ignorance – is perhaps the profoundest enactment of our connection with the world.
> In this pleasure we experience and celebrate our dependence and our gratitude, for we are living from mystery, from creatures we did not make and powers we cannot comprehend.
>
> Wendell Berry[99]

> Grace Before Meals
>
> ... Let us become aware of the memory
> Carried inside the food before us:
> The quiver of the seed
> Awakening in the earth, ...
> ... The kiss of rain and surge of sun ....
>
> –From "Grace Before Meals"
> by John O'Donohue[100]
> (The full prayer can be found at
> https://www.littlefreepantry.org/
> news/2018/11/14/grace-before-meals)

∗ Greet Other Beings

Imitate St. Francis, in your own way: say hello to other beings… your houseplants, the sun or moon as you step outside, trees and birds you see on your way to the car or public transit. Say something kind to him/her, like how beautiful she is, or how happy you are that he is there. You might like to call them brother or sister, like St. Francis, or you might use a different expression.

If there are other people around or you feel self-conscious, you can of course do this silently. If it seems awkward at first, be patient and give yourself time to get accustomed to this view of family.

If you have time, take a walk in nature one day with the intention of greeting other beings with appreciation and gratitude. First Nations people have the understanding that all beings are our relations. Of course, this is a Christian concept, too. We are all God's family. Take a moment to stand still, recognize that these are all your relations, and see yourself as part of this family of beings.

* As always, take time to quietly read the opening reflection for the next session. Read it through slowly and attentively. At the end of your reading, let what you have read sift through your mind. What do you still hold as a thought, an emotion, a reaction? What struck you in your reading. What moved you? Note what is stirring in your heart. Jot down some of your thoughts as you prepare for the next session.
* Recommended reading/viewing: BBC video, *Planet Earth*, segment on Grasslands.

Session 7

Human Landscape

Opening Reflection

John McCarthy, SJ

For some time, my favourite song was "I Still Haven't Found What I'm Looking For," by the Irish rock band U2. Released on U2's 1987 album, *The Joshua Tree*, the song became an instant hit. It is a haunting lament, a search for something more. Maybe it reminded me of a search for home, a longing for belonging. Refugees, migrants, the homeless, the displaced, the restless – we all seek a home. We all seek that domestic place of quiet and peace, the familiar and the sure. We all seek that haven of love and acceptance, of being rooted. We all seek a home.

Without a home, without a "fixed address," without a roof over our heads, we wander, restless, discontent, unsure of tomorrow, forgetful of yesterday, afraid for today. We need to belong.

The most fundamental of human desires – to seek family, place, and community – is manifest in our villages, our towns and cities, our farmscapes. Humans long to create a home, a physical home, but also a home of familiar patterns. We live in neighbourhoods. We create neighbourhoods of relationships, of walks, of boundaries. Our domstic abodes are expansive as we address the needs of our local neighbourhood, our city, our country, even the needs of our common home, the planet Earth. We create domestic place from exterior space.

At this point in our retreat process, we will focus on the environments that we have created, the spaces and places that offer us home and meaning. At this time, let us focus our prayer and reflection on the more immediate sense of home that we call neighbourhood, village, town, city, countryside, farmscape… We may be tempted to consider such built-up places as contrary to or opposed to the "natural world" that has been central to our reflections and prayer. This is understandable. Even our common word "forest" is rooted in the Latin *foris*, meaning "outside." The forest was that which existed outside the culture of town and village. The forest was the refuge of outlaws, given that the forest dwellers lived outside the place of civic law and order as defined by the city.[101]

My dad was a great fisherman. From the moment he could walk, I am sure that he was on the river with fishing pole in hand. Thankfully, he passed on to me that love of trouting in the rivers and ponds of Newfoundland. There was one river my dad seemed to love. The Colinet River, a small to medium-sized river by Newfoundland standards, flowed from the humid, foggy, coniferous forests of the central Avalon forests in eastern Newfoundland. Rich in sphagnum and mossy forests of fir and spruce, the forested uplands functioned as reservoirs of water that ran clean and strong to the North Atlantic Ocean.

Each summer, my dad would walk the hour or so across the neighbouring barrens and bogs to a certain bend in the river. The flow of the river over time had created a deep pool of steady water where the salmon would be found on their way upstream to the spawning grounds. Born in the Colinet River several years before, the Atantic salmon, having grown strong and free in the frigid Greenland waters of the North Atlantic, would find their way back home to that same river. Back to the river they came, intent on the continuation of life. It was in that pool in that bend in the river that Dad and the salmon would meet each year.

What drew both my dad and the salmon to that same river, to that same bend in the river, to that same pool in the same bend in the same river? A longing for home, perhaps.

For my dad, the river was home. In fact, I am sure it was his cathedral. It was where dad found his spirit. As the prophet Hosea professed, "Therefore, I will now allure her, and bring her into the wilderness, and speak tenderly to her" (Hosea 2:14). The *space* of the river became a *place* for my dad. Space and place. We take spaces for granted. But we transform spaces into places. Places are spaces imbued with meaning. Places are "interpreted, narrated, understood, felt, understood, and imagined."[102]

Tom McCarthy with Atlantic salmon, Colinet River, eastern Newfoundland, Canada (John McCarthy, SJ)

Dad's annual pilgrimage to the salmon pool (as well as the salmon's regular pilgrimage home) has created a river imbued with meaning, anticipated with hope, and celebrated in memory.

Do we not do the same with our neighbourhoods and built-up city- and townscapes? Or at least, should we not think of our surroundings in the same way as my dad loved the Colinet River and the salmon who lived it as home?

We make a home – a home that is physical and material. This is fundamental, the solid base upon which we root our lives. Apart from that, we create a home of familiar patterns, of customs, of traditions that root our memories. Christmas memories, for example, are rooted in family traditions and customs that ground us and offer us a solid foundation from which to thrive and live.

Home truly is where the heart is.

Session 7: Human Landscape

Preparation

* Video: "Home is Where the Heart Is" – from the 1962 film *Kid Galahad* (Elvis Presley) (3 min.). Available on YouTube.
* Video: *The Story of Jane Jacobs* (16 min.). Available on YouTube.
* Video: *Montrose Avenue* (5 min.). Available on Vimeo.
* Video: *Metropopular* (7 min.). Available on YouTube.

Opening Prayer (2 min.)

A Christian prayer in union with creation
(From *Laudato Si'*)

Father, we praise you with all your creatures.
They came forth from your all-powerful hand;
they are yours, filled with your presence and your tender love.
Praise be to you!

Son of God, Jesus,
through you all things were made.
You were formed in the womb of Mary our Mother,
you became part of this earth,
and you gazed upon this world with human eyes.
Today you are alive in every creature
in your risen glory.
Praise be to you!

Holy Spirit, by your light
you guide this world towards the Father's love
and accompany creation as it groans in travail.
You also dwell in our hearts
and you inspire us to do what is good.
Praise be to you!

Triune Lord, wondrous community of infinite love,
teach us to contemplate you
in the beauty of the universe,
for all things speak of you.
Awaken our praise and thankfulness
for every being that you have made.
Give us the grace to feel profoundly joined
to everything that is.

God of love, show us our place in this world
as channels of your love
for all the creatures of this earth,
for not one of them is forgotten in your sight.
Enlighten those who possess power and money
that they may avoid the sin of indifference,
that they may love the common good,
advance the weak,
and care for this world in which we live.
The poor and the earth are crying out.
O Lord, seize us with your power and light,
help us to protect all life,
to prepare for a better future,
for the coming of your Kingdom
of justice, peace, love and beauty.
Praise be to you!
Amen.

Exercise 1: Where Do You Feel Most at Home? (45 min.)

Listen to/watch the video "Home is Where the Heart Is," by Elvis Presley (easily found online).

Watch the video *Montrose Avenue.*

Reflection Questions

Take some quiet time in your seat or in some other quiet place. Reflect on the following three sets of questions:

1. Begin by imagining where you feel most at home. Who are the people with you? Where are you? What are you doing? What are your surroundings?

2. In the city, town, or village where you live, are there favourite places you like to visit? Sit there awhile. What feelings emerge when you bring these places to mind? What makes them so special to you? On the contrary, what are some places in your town or city where you do not like to visit or to be? Why is that so? When you think of your surroundings, what brings you sadness, doubt, or despair?
3. What creates a home for you? What is essential for you to call a place home?

Near the end of your meditation/reflection, write in your journal what comes to mind. How did the questions move you? Do you carry a thought or a feeling from the opening reflection offered for this session?

When you gather, be prepared to share one thing:

* Your favourite place where you live – your house, your neighbourhood, your city. What feelings, thoughts, and meaning do you associate with this place?

Exercise 2: Urban Centres, Jane Jacobs, and *Laudato Si'* (45 min.)

Read aloud the following section:

> Over 50% of the world's population (8.1 billion in 2024) live in cities. This trend is expected to continue. Increasingly, more people live in what we call megacities (cities with a population greater than 10 million inhabitants). The top three megacities are Tokyo (37 million), Delhi (33 million), and Shanghai (20 million). When compared to the population of Canada (about 40 million in 2024), the second-largest country in the world by land mass, the reality and challenges of megacities are readily apparent.
>
> Such population densities offer significant challenges for the governance and proper care of cities. Cities offer unlimited possibilities for human flourishing – employment, health care, arts and culture, education. Cities are intense cauldrons of great creativity and energy. At that same time, they can tumble into decline as impoverishment, lack of opportunity, poor security, pollution, and a host of other ailments take hold.

How do cities become home? What makes a city liveable?

To help us engage these questions, this session will consider the thought of Jane Jacobs (1916–2006), the author of arguably the most influential book on what makes cities liveable: *The Death and Life of Great American Cities* (published in 1961). Her ideas on urban renewal, radical at the time, eventually took hold as people sought how best to create liveable and flourishing cities.

This session will examine a short 16-minute video on the life and influence of Jane Jacobs. We will follow this with a reflective reading of excerpts from *Laudato Si'* where Pope Francis considers the ecology of our urban places. As we noted above in our reflection on the transformation of space into place, where we live, our environs, both acts as a source of meaning and is offered meaning by our daily lives over many years. We will conduct this session in several steps:

1. Watch the video *The Story of Jane Jacobs* (16 min.).
2. Read meditatively, on your own, the excerpts from *Laudato Si'* that deal with the places where we live. What word, phrase, or idea stands out for you?
3. Read the excerpts a second time. What now moves you?
4. Finally, read the excerpts a third time. What now resonates within you? Note your thoughts and ideas. Come prepared to share them with the group.
5. How do the thought of Jane Jacobs and that of Pope Francis compare?

Excerpts from "Decline in the Quality of Human Life and the Breakdown of Society" (*Laudato Si'*)

44. Nowadays, for example, we are conscious of the disproportionate and unruly growth of many cities, which have become unhealthy to live in, not only because of pollution caused by toxic emissions but also as a result of urban chaos, poor transportation, and visual pollution and noise. Many cities are huge, inefficient structures, excessively wasteful of energy and water. Neighbourhoods, even those recently built, are congested, chaotic and lacking in sufficient green space. We were not meant to be inundated by cement, asphalt, glass and metal, and deprived of physical contact with nature.

45. In some places, rural and urban alike, the privatization of certain spaces has restricted people's access to places of particular beauty. In others, "ecological" neighbourhoods have been created which are closed to outsiders in order to ensure an artificial tranquillity. Frequently, we find beautiful and carefully manicured green spaces in so-called "safer" areas of cities, but not in the more hidden areas where the disposable of society live.

Excerpts from "Ecology of Daily Life" (*Laudato Si'*)

147. Authentic development includes efforts to bring about an integral improvement in the quality of human life, and this entails considering the setting in which people live their lives. These settings influence the way we think, feel and act. In our rooms, our homes, our workplaces and neighbourhoods, we use our environment as a way of expressing our identity. We make every effort to adapt to our environment, but when it is disorderly, chaotic or saturated with noise and ugliness, such overstimulation makes it difficult to find ourselves integrated and happy.

148. An admirable creativity and generosity is shown by persons and groups who respond to environmental limitations by alleviating the adverse effects of their surroundings and learning to orient their lives amid disorder and uncertainty. For example, in some places, where the façades of buildings are derelict, people show great care for the interior of their homes, or find contentment in the kindness and friendliness of others. A wholesome social life can light up a seemingly undesirable environment. At times a commendable human ecology is practised by the poor despite numerous hardships. The feeling of asphyxiation brought on by densely populated residential areas is countered if close and warm relationships develop, if communities are created, if the limitations of the environment are compensated for in the interior of each person who feels held within a network of solidarity and belonging. In this way, any place can turn from being a hell on earth into the setting for a dignified life.

149. The extreme poverty experienced in areas lacking harmony, open spaces or potential for integration, can lead to incidents of brutality and to exploitation by criminal organizations. In the unstable neighbourhoods of mega-cities, the daily experience of overcrowding and social anonymity can create a sense of uprootedness which spawns antisocial behaviour and violence. Nonetheless, I wish to insist that love always proves more powerful. Many people in these conditions are able to weave bonds of belonging and togetherness which convert overcrowding into an experience of community in which the walls of the ego are torn down and the barriers of selfishness overcome. This experience of a communitarian salvation often generates creative ideas for the improvement of a building or a neighbourhood.

150. Given the interrelationship between living space and human behaviour, those who design buildings, neighbourhoods, public spaces and cities, ought to draw on the various disciplines which help us to understand

people's thought processes, symbolic language and ways of acting. It is not enough to seek the beauty of design. More precious still is the service we offer to another kind of beauty: people's quality of life, their adaptation to the environment, encounter and mutual assistance. Here too, we see how important it is that urban planning always take into consideration the views of those who will live in these areas.

151. There is also a need to protect those common areas, visual landmarks and urban landscapes which increase our sense of belonging, of rootedness, of "feeling at home" within a city which includes us and brings us together. It is important that the different parts of a city be well integrated and that those who live there have a sense of the whole, rather than being confined to one neighbourhood and failing to see the larger city as space which they share with others. Interventions which affect the urban or rural landscape should consider how various elements combine to form a whole which is perceived by its inhabitants as a coherent and meaningful framework for their lives. Others will then no longer be seen as strangers, but as part of a "we" which all of us are working to create. For this same reason, in both urban and rural settings, it is helpful to set aside some places which can be preserved and protected from constant changes brought by human intervention.

152. Lack of housing is a grave problem in many parts of the world, both in rural areas and in large cities, since state budgets usually cover only a small portion of the demand. Not only the poor, but many other members of society as well, find it difficult to own a home. Having a home has much to do with a sense of personal dignity and the growth of families. This is a major issue for human ecology. In some places, where makeshift shanty towns have sprung up, this will mean developing those neighbourhoods rather than razing or displacing them. When the poor live in unsanitary slums or in dangerous tenements, "in cases where it is necessary to relocate them, in order not to heap suffering upon suffering, adequate information needs to be given beforehand, with choices of decent housing offered, and the people directly involved must be part of the process". At the same time, creativity should be shown in integrating rundown neighbourhoods into a welcoming city: "How beautiful those cities which overcome paralyzing mistrust, integrate those who are different and make this very integration a new factor of development! How attractive are those cities which, even in their architectural design, are full of spaces which connect, relate and favour the recognition of others!"

153. The quality of life in cities has much to do with systems of transport, which are often a source of much suffering for those who use them. Many cars, used by one or more people, circulate in cities, causing traffic congestion, raising the level of pollution, and consuming enormous quantities of non-renewable energy. This makes it necessary to build more roads and parking areas whichspoil the urban landscape. Many specialists agree on the need to give priority to public transportation. Yet some measures needed will not prove easily acceptable to society uless substantial improvements are made in the systems themselves, which in many cities force people to put up with undignified conditions due to crwding, inconvenience, infrequent service and lack of safety.

154. Respect for our dignity as human beings often jars with the chaotic realities that people must endure in city life. Yet this should not make us overlook the abandonment and neglect also experienced by some rural populations whichlack access to essential services and where some workers are reduced to conditions of servitude, without rights or even the hope of a more dignified life.

Exercise 3: A Final Reflection on Home and Place (10 min.)

Nan Sheppard (1893–1981) was a celebrated Scottish writer and poet. She is best remembered for her 1977 seminal work entitled *The Living Mountain*,[103] which continues to be enjoyed and relished today. The fruit of years of mountain walking the Cairngorms of northeast Scotland, what Robert McFarlane calls "Britain's Arctic,"[104] her soulful reflections reach to the mountain places, to the point where "place and a mind may interpenetrate till the nature of both is altered."[105] A contemporary Scottish writer, Amanda Thomson, rooting herself in the Caledonian pinewoods of northern Scotland, in the tradition of Sheppard ends her reflections on the natural histories of place, identity, and home with a simple declaration: "This is where I choose to live, choose to stay."[106]

In your life, where have you chosen to live? Where have you chosen to stay? How have those decisions (or lack of decisions) marked your life? What factors determined where you now live? Take some time to sit in silence with these qustions. In your journal, jot down your reflections. Let them rest with you this week.

Exercise 4: City Stereotypes (10 min.)

Watch *Metropopular* — a charming animated short film exploring stereotypes of US cities through an imagined dialogue between anthropomorphized metropolises.

Closing Prayer (2 min.)

Loving God,
Creator of Heaven, Earth, and all therein contained.
Open our minds and touch our hearts,
so that we can be part of Creation, your gift.
Be present to those in need in these difficult times,
especially the poorest and most vulnerable. …
Make us courageous in embracing the changes
required to seek the common good.
Now more than ever, may we all feel
interconnected and interdependent.

Enable us to succeed in listening and responding to
the cry of the Earth and the cry of the poor.
May their current sufferings become the birth-
pangs of a more fraternal and sustainable world.

We pray through Christ our Lord, under the loving
gaze of Mary Help of Christians.

Amen.[107]

Continuing Your Prayer at Home

∗ Pray your neighbourhood

How we view our lives may be quite different from how the Holy Trinity views our lives. The Ignatian Examen, a review of one's day in the light of the Holy Spirit, may help us to see the day that has passed in the light of the love and mercy of God. We can do a similar prayer for our neighbourhood. How we see our neighbourhood, how we relate to our neighbourhood, determines whether we feel at home or not. How we consider our neighbourhood or neighbours may be quite different from how God sees our neighbourhood and our neighbours. What may God be calling us to consider, to change, to promote in our neighbourhood or community? What follows is an invitation to "pray your neighbourhood." Let it become a habit, a way of "praying always" as you move about town or city. Consider how you are being changed as you pray the place where you live.

1. Choose your route

As you start your walk ask God to go with you. You can decide ahead of time where you're going to walk, or you can simply ask th Holy Spirit to lead you as you go. Just make sure you don't get lost!

2. Keep your eyes and ears open

Pay attention to the people you pass, as well as the landscape and atmosphere of the places through which you walk. Pause and pray outside hospitals, schools, local government buildings and other places of influence. Ask God to draw your attention to things He wants you to pray for.

3. Pray the positive

Focus on God's love for the people and the place. Pray blessing, even (especially!) in areas that are considered 'dark' or 'difficult.' Use The Lord's Prayer: "Your Kingdom come, your will be done..." (Matt. 6:10)

4. Look for God's fingerprints

Ask God to show you where He is already at work in a place. Listen for Bible verses [that come to mind] and promises to pray over the area.

5. Make notes

Record what you notice, what you pray for and any verses, pictures, or words you believe God spoke to you. When you pray for the area again, read these notes before you begin.[108]

* As always, take time to quietly read the opening reflection for the next session. Read it through slowly and attentively. At the end of your reading, let what you have read sift through your mind. What do you still hold as a thought, an emotion, a reaction? What struck you in your reading? What moved you? Note what is stirring in your heart. Jot down some of your thoughts as you prepare for the next session.

Session 8

Coming Full Circle, Deeper in the Love of God

Opening Reflection

Yvonne Prowse

A direct connection exists between the heart of a person and all the elements of the cosmos.

—St. Hildegard of Bingen[109]

"Abide in me as I abide in you."
[Jesus, speaking at the Last Supper]

(John 15:4)

Shortly before sunset one summer evening, after hiking in the Sierra Nevada mountains, I was sitting on a patio at a restaurant awaiting dinner. Gently, but suddenly, I was filled with a sense of oneness with the world, a sense of deep, inherent connectedness to all creation. Despite my awareness of so many struggles and so much pain in the world – wars, poverty, and abuse – I was immersed in a sense of light and serenity… an utter assurance of Love present, infusing everything and everyone. With it came deep knowing or experiencing that somehow, under or embracing all the horrors and suffering, all is right with the world. This awareness lasted several minutes and then gently subsided, and I returned to "ordinary" time and space, but changed by this experience.

Rocky Mountains, Alberta, Canada (Yvonne Prowse)

Was this what Jesus meant when he said, "The kingdom of God is at hand"? Is it what Julian of

Norwich understood when she heard God say, "All shall be well, and all manner of things shall be well"? I am not sure, though they resonated in me as I reflected on it.

Virgin River, Zion National Park, Utah (Yvonne Prowse)

While it was an extraordinary moment, I do not think it was uncommon. Many of us have experiences where "the veil" is thin. Sometimes a person is moed so profoundly that it changes everything – like Thomas Merton's experience standing on a street corner in Louisville and realizing he loved everyone. Often these moments are quieter, gentler, perhaps not asking for us to change much. I have heard people describe various moments in which it seemed the world opened up, or was infused with light and love, or God felt utterly present, or they had a sense of being embraced by God, or a feeling of utter belonging. People have spoken of such experiences occurring at sunset… or holding their newborn child… or suddenly seeing their spouse with a full sense of love and appreciation… or a sense of immersion in God while swimming or listening to music…

Sitting by the Cardoner River in Spain, St. Ignatius of Loyola had a profound experience: "the eyes of his understanding began to be opened; not that he saw any vision, but he understood … many things … and this was so great an enlightenment that everything seemed new to him."[110] I think he, too, found such experiences of the divine difficult to put into words. I also believe he knew that they are not uncommon. He ends his *Spiritual Exercises* with a prayer that invites us to recall such moments where the veil is thin, when we sense God so close in the life around us – and also, perhaps, to lead us into a new moment of this kind, or at least to have a glimpse, a taste.

For our last session of this retreat, we do not consider a new landscape. Rather, we come full circle, but a level lower, deeper into God's heart, deeper into love, hopefully, with creation. We will, in this last session, take up the prayer mentioned above to lead us deeper into the heart of God.

In preparation for the last session, take a bit of time to reflect on your life and recall any moment when you felt the veil between the worlds was thin… when you sensed God so very close, or a deep sense of peace, love, protection… a moment when some kindness shifted your perspective and freed you… a moment of laughter that connected you to someone or something or to yourself… Any moment of awe fits. Awe is a direct connection with the Holy. You may recall just one moment that you want to spend a bit of time remembering, savouring. Or there may be several. If the memories are slow to come, turn to God, to Jesus, and ask what they remember.

If you have a bit of time another day, reflect on what you have experienced over this retreat. Begin to gather the graces o the retreat – the ways in which you wre blessed, healed, heard, affirmed, renewed. Notice what has changed in you over the time of this retreat and the ways in which you – your thoughts, fears, hopes, feelings – were transformed.

This may be a suitable time to recall some of St. Paul's words to the people of Corinth: "You are a new creation in Christ" (2 Corinthians 5:17). Also, call to mind Jesus' assurance that "With God all things are possible" (Mark 10:27).

Session 8: Coming Full Circle, Deeper in the Love of God

Preparation

- A large bow of sand to serve as a stand for taper candles
- Taper candles (1 for each participant)
- Or use a large bowl of water and floating candles
- An audio recording of "The Deer's Cry" and equipment to play it (no visual necessary). Rita Connelly's iconic version can be found on YouTube.

Opening Prayer (3 min.)Play "The Deer's Cry" – just audio, no visual necessary.

Or, if the recording is not available, read aloud the lyrics, which come from the popular prayer "St. Patrick's Breastplate."[111]

Exercise 1: Prayer with *Contemplatio*[112]

(25 min. + 20 min. for sharing)

Introduction (read aloud in the group):

We began this retreat praying with the story of our emerging universe and with our own personal blessed history. It was said then that:

> The life story of each of us can be seen as an experience of the Trinity's love coming to us through the life of Jesus, and through … friends, family, the living creatures sharing Earth with us, and the actual mineral substances of our earth.[113]

We now approach that truth anew as we gather all that has occurred in our earts and minds in this retreat. St. Ignatius ends his Spiritual Exercises with a beautiful prayer called the "Contemplation on Love." It is also a contemplation on "the mystery of my own life within the community of all life."[114]

To begin it, Ignatius calls our attention to two things:

- First, love ought to be manifested more in deeds than words. [SpExx 230]
- Second, love consists in mutual sharing between people. For example, the one who loves gives and shares with the beloved what he/she possesses or has to give; and vice versa, the beloved shares with the lover. Thus, if one has knowledge, one gives to the other who does not, and so also with honours and riches. Each shares with the other. [SpExx 231]

It is helpful to keep these in mind during this prayer.

This contemplation is done in silence. The group may disperse for each participant to find a quiet place to pray; or play some peaceful instrumental music while the group sits together in silent prayer.

The Prayer[115] (to be done individually, in silence or with peaceful music playing)

To begin:

I imagine that I am standing in the presence of the Trinity, with Jesus Christ and all the blessed and saintly beings, both great and small, of the universe, smiling on me.

I ask God for a deep, intimate knowledge of having been so blessed by God's love that I will be filled with gratitude and impelled to love and serve God in all things.

1. I recall the creativity of the Trinity in thevast evolutionary process which results in the formation of millions of galaxies, stars, planets, as well as me and my loved ones. I further recall *all the gifts and blessings* with which the Trinity has been so good to me, including

God's presence in special people and occasions in my life, special creatures, and places. I ponder, with deep feeling, how much the Trinity has done for me and for all the community of life; how much they have given me; and how much more they desire to give, how much they desire to give me their very selves.

I want to love in return. I make my offering as fully as I can, saying the following prayer:

Take under your protection, [O God],
my entire freedom.
Receive my memory, my intellect,
and all of my will.
Whatever I have or possess,
You have lavished on me:
to You I return it all,
and surrender it to be governed totally
by your will.
Give me only love of You, together with
your grace,
and I am rich enough, and ask for
nothing more.[116]

2. I see how *the Trinity dwells in these gifts and blessings*... God dwells in all creation; in the elements, giving them existence; in the plants, giving them life; in the animals, giving them sensation; in human beings, giving them understanding. I sense this reality in me – God giving me being... life... sensation... understanding.... God dwells in me. I am the image of God. I remain present until I am drawn to return God's love... to give myself in love, praying the same prayer as above...

   ... *Take under your protection, O God...*

3. I perceive how *God labours in these gifts*; with all the beings and matter of the universe, all the landscapes, the Trinity labours and works for me, in me, and continues their creativity in me. For example, they are working in the heavens, elements, plants, fruits, cattle... the prairies, deserts, forests – giving them their existence, protecting them, giving growth and feeling. I reflect on myself and again desire to give myself in love... *Take under your protection, O God...*

4. I reflect on how *everything descends from above* and is a radiance, a participation of God... my power, a radiance of infinite power... my goodness, a radiance of infinite goodness... my compassion, my beauty, my justice... each a radiance of God... like rays from the sun... or the rains from their source. I am a part of God and creation, and they are a part of me. Again, I desire to give myself in love... *Take under your protection, O God...*

To draw to a close:

I talk with Jesus and listen as dear friends speak with one another; I tell him what is in my heart and listen to his heart. With him I consider how this prayer, and this retreat, have moved me to care for and be in relationship with creation, with Earth.

Finish with *Take under your protection, O God*, or the Our Father.

Before rejoining the group, consider what you wish to share: two or three points from this prayer that are most significant to you, that you want to honour, claim, remember...

Sharing (20 min.)

Share in groups of 4 to 6 people.

Round #1: Each person shares as they wish.

Round #2: What commonalities do you notice in the group?

Break (10 min.)

Exercise 2: Gathering Graces of the Retreat (55 min.)

1. Sharing in Pairs Using Open Sentences (25 min.)

There will be two rounds of pairings, each with three open sentences. After the first round, change the pairings for three new open sentences. Each person has 2 minutes to share and should speak for the whole 2 minutes.

The facilitator keeps time for the whole group.

In the first pairing, choose who goes first in some random way, such as the person with the darker eyes shares first. Do not leave it up to the pairs to decide, as this can be distracting. Their partner listens attentively, without speaking. When 2 minutes is up, that person stops speaking, and the partner shares, beginning with the same open sentence.

For the second sentence, the partner who shared second before shares first now.

In this retreat, the landscape that most moved me was...

One of the ways I experienced God's love in this retreat was...

One source of pain – grief, anger, fear – for the world that came up for me in this retreat was...

For the second pairing, everyone switches to new partners. Select another random way of choosing who shares first.

Something that really changed in me in this retreat is...

Something I am moved to do differently as a result of this retreat is...

Some part of Earth that I fell in love with during this retreat is...

2. Sharing in the Large Group (30 min.)

Each person shares:

* one of the most significant graces I received during this retreat
* a notable change that has occurred in my relationship with creation – this may be a hange in perspective, attitude, behaviour
* how I want to manifest that change in my care for our common home

Each person lights a candle and places it in the bowl of sand or water (before, during, or after their sharing).

When the person is done, the group responds together with a phrase such as "We bless you, _(name)__" or "__(nae)__, we hold you in our hearts." Respond for each person in kind.

Close this exercise with the facilitator reading a blessing – the one below or another of your choosing:

For Movement as One

Michelle Fraser

May we sense the direction of the universe.

May we feel in our depths the rhythms
and movements
Of endless expansion.

May our communal pulse
Root us and propel us into right action

May the momentum of Earth launch us
As we absorb her energy and release our
selves in service –
Melting, leaping, soaring in joy.

May our inner peace and freedom
Flow together with the stream of life,
Carrying nourishment and pure water
To the infinite sea.[117]

Any Final Business

Here the facilitator or participants can mention any final housekeeping or other comments before the retreat concludes with a prayer.

Closing Prayer (2 min.)

Pray aloud in the group – in unison or antiphonally (i.e., half the group reads stanza a; the other half reads stanza b; and so on).

To a God Whose Name Is Love[118]

(a) What return can I make to you, Love?
for all your goodness to me?
I will take up the cu of sharing;
I will bless your bountiful name.
I will do what I vowed to you, Love,
in the presence of all creation.

(b) What return can I mke to you, Love?
for always dwelling in me?
I will take up the cup of welcome;
I will image your indwelling name.
I will do what I vowed to you, Love,
in the body of all creation.

(c) What return can I make to you, Love?
for all your labor for me?
I will offer the gift of my life;
I will live for your name.
I will do what I vowed to you, ove,
by my work for all creation.

(d) What return can I make to you, Love?
for your infinite love filling me?
I will love with the love of creating;
I will make new your name.
I will fulfill what I vowed to you, Love,
in completing your gift of creation.

Left to right: Bryce Canyon National Park, Utah (Yvonne Prowse); Boreal forest, Orphan Lake Trail, Ontario, Canada (Trevor Scott, SJ); Killarney, Ontario, Canada (Trevor Scott, SJ); Great Sand Dunes National Park and Preserve, Colorado (Trevor Scott, SJ)

Endnotes

1 Norman Wirzba, *From Nature to Creation: A Christian Vision for Understanding and Loving our World* (Grand Rapids, MI: Baker Academic, 2015).

2 N. Max Wildiers, *The Theologian and His Universe: Theology and Cosmology from the Middle Ages to the Present* (New York: The Seabury Press, 1982).

3 Louis Dupré, *Passage to Modernity: An Essay in the Hermeneutics of Nature and Culture* (New Haven, CT: Yale University Press, 1993).

4 John F. Haught, *Is Nature Enough? Meaning and Truth in the Age of Science* (Cambridge, MA: Cambridge University Press, 2006), 6.

5 John W. McCarthy and Nancy C. Tuchman, "How We Speak of Nature: A Plea for a Discourse of Depth," *The Heythrop Journal* 59:6 (2018): 944–58.

6 Douglas E. Christie, *The Blue Sapphire of the Mind: Notes for a Contemplative Ecology* (New York: Oxford University Press, 2013), 3.

7 Christie, *Blue Sapphire,* 3–4.

8 *Laudato Si'*: Encyclical letter of the Holy Father Francis on Care for our Common Home (2015), #11.

9 Pierre Dansereau, *Inscape and Landscape: The Human Perception of Environment* (New York: Columbia University Press, 1973).

10 Blaise Pascal, *Pensées* (Mineola, NY: Dover Publications, 2003), 78.

11 Erazim Kohák, *The Embers and the Stars: A Philosophical Inquiry into the Moral Sense of Nature* (Chicago: University of Chicago Press, 1984), 207.

12 Kohák, *Embers and Stars,* 210.

13 Simon Schama, *Landscape and Memory* (Toronto: Random House of Canada, 1995).

14 Schama, *Landscape and Memory,* 14.

15 Denis Edwards, *Ecology at the Heart of Faith: The Change of Heart that Leads to a New Way of Living on Earth* (Maryknoll, NY: Orbis Books, 2006).

16 Langdon Gilkey, *Maker of Heaven and Earth: The Christian Doctrine of Creation in the Light of Modern Knowledge* (Lanham, MD: University Press of America, 1985); Paul M. Blowers, *Drama of the Divine Economy: Creator and Creation in Early Christian Theology and Piety,* ed. Gillian Clark and Andrew Louth, Oxford Early Christian Studies (Oxford: Oxford University Press, 2012).

17 Brian D. Robinette, *The Difference Nothing Makes: Creation, Christ, Contemplation* (Notre Dame, IN: University of Notre Dame Press, 2023); Gary A. Anderson and Markus Bockmuehl, eds., *Creation* ex nihilo: *Origins, Development, Contemporary Challenges* (Notre Dame, IN: University of Notre Dame Press, 2018); Ian A. McFarland, *From Nothing: A Theology of Creation* (Louisville, KY: Westminster John Knox Press, 2014).

18 *Catechism of the Catholic Church,* Section two (on creation), para. 4, "The Creator."

19 *Laudato Si',* #233.

20 Blowers, *Drama Divine Economy,* 1–17.

21 Blowers, *Drama Divine Economy,* 222–41.

22 Elizabeth A. Johnson, "Jesus and the Cosmos: Soundings in Deep Christology," in *Incarnation: On the Scope and Depth of Christology,* ed. Niels Henrik Gregersen (Minneapolis: Fortress Press, 2015), 133–56.

23 Charles Darwin, *The Origin of Species by Means of Natural Selection or the Preservation of Favored Races in the Struggle for Life,* The Modern Library ed. (New York: Random House, 1993, 1859), 648–49.

24 Catherine Mowry LaCugna, *God for Us: The Trinity and Christian Life* (San Francisco: HarperSanFrancisco, 1991), 271.

25 Edwards, *Ecology at the Heart of Faith,* 65–81.

26 Camilo Mora et al., "How Many Species Are There on Earth and in the Ocean?" *PLOS Biology* 9, no. 8 (2011), https://doi.org/10.1371/journal.pbio.1001127; John J. Wiens, "How Many Species Are There on Earth? Progress and Problems," *PLOS Biology* 21, no. 11 (2023), https://doi.org/10.1371/journal.pbio.3002388.

27 *Laudato Si',* #238.

28 Paul O'Callaghan, *God's Gift of the Universe: An Introduction to Creation Theology* (Washington, DC: The Catholic University of America Press, 2022), 198–212.

29 "For redeemed by Christ and made a new creature in the Holy Spirit, man is able to love the things themselves created by God, and ought to do so. He can receive them from God and respect and reverence them as flowing constantly from the hand of God" (*Gaudium et Spes* #37); "The faithful … must learn the deepest meaning and the value of all creation, as well as its role in the harmonious praise of God" (*Lumen Gentium* #36); "The Church, to which we are all called in Christ Jesus, and in which we acquire sanctity through the grace of God, will attain its full perfection only in the glory of heaven, when there will come the time of the restoration of all things. At that time the human race as well as the entire world, which is intimately related to man and attains to its end through him, will be perfectly reestablished in Christ" (*Lumen Gentium* #48).

30 "For by the very circumstance of their having been created, all things are endowed with their own stability, truth, goodness, proper laws and order" (*Gaudium et Spes* #36).

31 Rachel Carson, *Silent Spring* (Boston: Houghton Mifflin, 1962).

32 *Octogesima Adveniens* (1971), #21.

33 Message of His Holiness Pope John Paul II for the celebration of the World Day of Peace, 1 January 1990, *Peace with God the Creator, Peace with All of Creation,* #15.

34 John Paul II, *Peace with God the Creator,* #16.

35 Jean Bastaire, ed., *Jean-Paul II: Les gémissements de la création – Vingt textes sur l'écologie* (Paris: Éditions Parole et Silence, 2006); Woodeene Koenig-Bricker, *Ten Commandments for the Environment: Pope Benedict XVI Speaks Out for Creation and Justice* (Notre Dame, IN: Ave Maria Press, 2009); Maria Milvia Morciano, ed., *Pope Benedict XVI: The Garden of God – Toward a Human Ecology* (Washington, DC: The Catholic University of America Press, 2014); *The Environment: Pope Benedict XVI,* ed. Jacquelyn Lindsey (Huntington, IN: Our Sunday Visitor, 2012).

36 Pontifical Council for Justice and Peace, *Compendium of the Social Doctrine of the Church* (Città del Vaticano: Libreria Editrice Vaticana, 2004).

37 Among a growing literature of eco-theology, the following works are but a sampling. Margaret Barker, *Creation: A Biblical Vision for the Environment* (London: T&T Clark International, 2010); Richard Bauckham, *The Bible and Ecology: Rediscovering the Community of Creation* (Waco, TX: Baylor University Press, 2010); Thomas Berry, *The Dream of the Earth* (San Francisco: Sierra Club Books, 1988); John Chryssavgis and Bruce V. Foltz, eds., *Toward an Ecology of Transfiguration: Orthodox Christian Perspectives on Environment, Nature, and Creation* (New York: Fordham University Press, 2013); Celia Deane-Drummond, *Ecotheology* (London: Darton, Longman and Todd, 2008); Elizabeth A. Johnson, *Ask the Beasts: Darwin and the God of Love* (London: Bloomsbury, 2014); Jame Schaefer, *Theological Foundations for Environmental Ethics: Reconstructing Patristic and Medieval Concepts* (Washington, DC: Georgetown University Press, 2009); Frederiek Depoortere and Jacques Haers, eds., *To Discern Creation in a Scattering World,* Bibliotheca Ephemeridum Theologicarum Lovaniensium CCLXII (Leuven: Uitgeverij Peeters, 2013); Denis Edwards, ed., *Earth Revealing – Earth Healing: Ecology and Christian Theology* (Collegeville, MN: Liturgical Press, 2001).

38 Social Affairs Commission, Canadian Conference of Catholic Bishops, "'You love all that exists … *all things are Yours, God, lover of life*': A Pastoral Letter on the Christian Imperative," October 4, 2003.

39 Social Affairs Commission, Canadian Conference of Catholic Bishops, *Our Relationship with the Environment: The Need for Conversion,* 2008.

40 Rebecca Rathbone and Simon Appolloni, eds., *Generation Laudato Si': Catholic Youth on Living Out an Ecological Spirituality* (Toronto: Novalis, 2023).

41 *Laudato Si',* #137.

42 *Laudato Si',* #139.

43 Maya Angelou, *I Know Why the Caged Bird Sings* (New York: Random House, 1969).

44 SpExx = Spiritual Exercises of St. Ignatius of Loyola.

45 Joanna Macy and Molly Young Brown, *Coming Back to Life* (Gabriola Island, BC: New Society Publishers, 2014), 77.

46 John O'Donohue, *Walking in Wonder: Eternal Wisdom for a Modern World* (New York: Convergent Books, 2015), 49, 56.

47 We are not simply placed on Earth, but are beings of Earth, and live *in* her biosphere.

48 J. Philip Newell, *Celtic Benediction: Morning and Night Prayer* (Ottawa: Novalis, 2000), 22.

49 John English, SJ, Lois Zachariah and Kuruvila Zachariah, "Twenty-four Spiritual Exercises for the New Story of Universal Communion," *Progressio* Supplement no. 57 (November 2002), 140.

50 Jacqueline Bergan and S. Marie Schwan, 1985, quoted in Katherine Dyckman, Mary Garvin, and Elizabeth Liebert, *The Spiritual Exercises Reclaimed: Uncovering Liberating Possibilities for Women* (Mahwah, NJ: Paulist Press, 2001).

51 John English, SJ, "Dialoguing with the Dance of Creation," *The Way* 43, no. 1 (January 2004): 24.

52 John English, SJ, Lois Zachariah and Kuruvila Zachariah, "Twenty-four Spiritual Exercises for the New Story of Universal Communion," *Progressio* Supplement, no. 57 (November 2002), 43.

53 I have been praying with and sharing the Universe Story in various formats for several years. This version is compiled from various sources, including "God Creating," an annual retreat talk given by Bill Clarke, SJ at Loyola House in Guelph, Ontario; "The New Story," a talk given by James Profit, SJ at Providence Spirituality Centre; "The Stations of the Cosmos" installation on the land of Ignatius Jesuit Centre, Guelph, and its accompanying guide-brochure, which I edited; and the following books: Denis Edwards, *Ecology at the Heart of Faith* (Maryknoll, NY: Orbis Books, 2008); Brian Swimme, *The Universe Is a Green Dragon* (Rochester, VT: Bear & Co., 2001); Brian Swimme, *The Hidden Heart of the Cosmos* (Maryknoll, NY: Orbis Books, 1996).

54 Julian of Norwich, *Revelations of Divine Love,* the short text, chapter 5, trans. Elizabeth Spearing (London: Penguin Books, 1998).

55 Elizabeth A. Johnson, CSJ, "An Earthy Christology: 'For God So Loved the Cosmos,'" *America,* April 13, 2009, 29.

56 Elizabeth Johnson, *Creation and the Cross: The Mercy of God for a Planet in Peril* (Maryknoll, NY: Orbis Books, 2018), 199.

57 "A Prayer for the Earth: Laudato Si'," EcoJesuit website, https://www.ecojesuit.com/prayer-for-the-earth-video-from-laudato-si.

58 *The Message Bible: The Bible in Contemporary Language,* https://messagebible.com.

59 Paraphrased from "The Water Crisis," Drop in the Bucket website, https://dropinthebucket.org/water-facts/?gad_source=1&gclid=EAIaIQobChMI2bKzpuS4hAMV6DbUAR3QYgOWEAAYASA

AEgI0W_D_BwE, and United Nations, "Water: At the Centre of the Climate Crisis," https://www.un.org/en/climatechange/science/climate-issues/water?gad_source=1&gclid=EAIaIQobChMI2bKzpuS4hAMV6DbUAR3QYgOWEAAYAiAAEgLiKvD_BwE.

60 Quoted in "Living Water: The Spiritual Ecology of Water," Jesuit Forum for Social Faith and Justice, *Open Space* 14, no. 3 (May 2022), 6, https://jesuitforum.ca/resources/open-space.

61 Paraphrased from United Nations, "Water: At the Centre of the Climate Crisis."

62 Quoted in "Living Water: The Spiritual Ecology of Water," Jesuit Forum for Social Faith and Justice, *Open Space* 14, no. 3 (May 2022), 4, https://jesuitforum.ca/resources/open-space.

63 Paraphrased from United Nations, "Water: At the Centre of the Climate Crisis."

64 Quoted in "Living Water: The Spiritual Ecology of Water," 3, Jesuit Forum for Social Faith and Justice, *Open Space* 14, no. 3 (May 2022), https://jesuitforum.ca/resources/open-space.

65 "Reconciling God, Creation and Humanity: An Ignatian Examen," https://www.ecologicalexamen.org.

66 National Geographic, "Mind the Water Gap," https://worldwatermap.nationalgeographic.org.

67 c. 2017 Nancy Wood Literary Trust, www.NancyWood.com. First published in Hollering Sun, 1972.

68 Graham McDowell, Madison Stevens, Shawn Marshall, et al., *Canadian Mountain Assessment: Walking Together to Embrace Understanding of Mountains in Canada* (Calgary: University of Calgary Press, 2023). This book is available as an Open Access E-Book.

69 Helen Pike, "New Collaborative Publication Puts Mountains on the Map for Canadians," CBC News, Nov. 6, 2023, https://www.cbc.ca/news/canada/calgary/canadian-mountain-assessment-1.7018922.

70 Bob Dufford, SJ, "Sing to the Mountains," https://hymnary.org/text/i_will_give_thanks_to_you_my_lord.

71 John Paul II, *Catechesis* (30 January 2002), 6: Insegnamenti 25/1 (2002), 140.

72 Social Affairs Commission, Canadian Conference of Catholic Bishops, "You love all that exists…," 1.

73 Taizé, "O Lord, Hear My Prayer," https://hymnary.org/text/o_lord_hear_my_prayer_o_lord_hear.

74 John Bell, "Take, O Take Me as I Am," https://hymnary.org/text/take_o_take_me_as_i_am.

75 Folliott Sandford Pierpoint, "For the Beauty of the Earth," https://hymnary.org/text/for_the_beauty_of_the_earth.

76 S. Gauthier et al., "Boreal Forest Health and Global Change," *Science* 349, no. 6250 (2015), 819–22.

77 Jeffery V. Wells et al., "The State of Conservation in North America's Boreal Forest: Issues and Opportunities," *Frontiers in Forests and Global Change* 3 (2020), https://doi.org/https://doi.org/10.3389/ffgc.2020.00090.

78 Adapted from John McCarthy, SJ, *Do Monkeys Go to Heaven? 2.0: More Reflections on Finding God in All Creation* (Toronto: Novalis, 2017), 29.

79 Robert Pogue Harrison, *Forests: The Shadow of Civilization* (Chicago: University of Chicago Press, 1992), 247.

80 Taizé, "O Lord, Hear My Prayer," https://hymnary.org/text/o_lord_hear_my_prayer_o_lord_hear.

81 Wilfred Thesiger, https://www.goodreads.com/author/quotes/169954.Wilfred_Thesiger.

82 Edward Abbey, *Desert Solitaire: A Season in the Wilderness* (New York: Ballantine Books, 1985), 7.

83 "Anselm Kiefer Interview with Michael Auping," Oct. 5, 2004, http://www.neugraphic.com/kiefer/kiefer-text1.html.

84 Judith Benhamou Reports, "The Confessions of Anselm Kiefer, the Star of Painting," undated, https://judithbenhamouhuet.com/the-confessions-of-anselm-kiefer-the-star-of-painting-today.

85 Eugene H. Peterson, The Message: *The Bible in Contemporary Language* (Colorado Springs: NavPress, 2002).

86 "A Prayer in the Desert," https://faithhub.net/a-prayer-in-the-desert-ready-for-skye.

87 Christina Nunez, "Grasslands, Explained," *National Geographic*, Mar. 15, 2019, https://www.nationalgeographic.com/environment/article/grasslands.

88 Terry Tempest Williams, *Finding Beauty in a Broken World* (New York: Random House, 2008), 89.

89 Williams, *Finding Beauty in a Broken World*, 44–46.

90 Quoted in Judy Cannato, *Radical Amazement: Contemplative Lessons from Black Holes, Supernovas, and Other Wonders of the Universe* (Notre Dame, IN: Sorin Books, 2006), 7.

91 "When Studying Ecology Means Celebrating Its Gifts," Science Friday website, Oct. 28, 2022, https://www.sciencefriday.com/segments/braiding-sweetgrass-land-book.

92 Hermann Hesse, "Sometimes" in *Earth Prayers*, ed. Elizabeth Roberts and Elisa Amidon (San Francisco: Harper San Francisco 1991). Full poem available at https://inwardboundpoetry.blogspot.com/2020/06/1044-sometimes-hermann-hesse.html

93 William H. Draper, "All Creatures of Our God and King," https://hymnary.org/text/all_creatures_of_our_god_and_king.

94 St. Francis composed this song of praise in 1225, and it is considered the first poem in vernacular Italian. Pope Francis's 2015 encyclical *Laudato Si'* takes its name and inspiration from St. Francis's work. The title means "Praise Be to You" in medieval Italian, a phrase that is repeated throughout the Canticle. Source:

The Franciscan Friars, Franciscan Ministries and Missions (franciscanfriarscresson.org).

95 I first learned these questions in a weekend workshop with Macy in Guelph around 2015. When I did her exercise at that time, it was topsoil that came to me and spoke.

96 Wendell Berry, "The Gift of Good Land," in *The Gift of Good Land: Further Essays Cultural and Agricultural* (New York: North Point Press, 1981), 281.

97 I am especially grateful to three sources for my development of this ritual: Kathleen Duffy, SSJ, "The Eucharist as Liturgical Drama: Teilhard's 'The Mass on the World,'" in *Personal Transformation and a New Creation: The Spiritual Revolution of Beatrice Brutea,* ed. Ilia Delio (Maryknoll, NY: Orbis Books, 2017); Thomas M. King, SJ, *Teilhard's Mass: Approaches to "The Mass on the World"* (Mahwah, NJ: Paulist Press, 2005); and Hugh O'Donnell, *Eucharist and the Living Bread* (Dublin: Columba Press, 2012).

98 Sr. Miriam Therese MacGillis, "Food as Sacrament," in *Bread, Body and Spirit: Finding the Sacred in Food,* ed. Alice Peck (Woodstock, VT: SkyLight Paths, 2008), 9–10.

99 Wendell Berry, *What Are People For? Essays,* 2nd ed. (New York: Counterpoint, 2010), 152.

100 John O'Donohue, *To Bless the Space Between Us: A Book of Blessings* (New York: Random House, 2008), 91.

101 Robert Pogue Harrison, *Forests: The Shadow of Civilization* (Chicago: University of Chicago Press, 1992), 69–81.

102 Thomas F. Gieryn, "A space for place in sociology," *Annual Review of Sociology* 26 (2000), 465. See also William P. Stewart, Daniel R. Williams, and Linda E. Kruger, eds., *Place-Based Conservation: Perspectives from the Social Sciences* (Dordrecht: Springer, 2013).

103 Nan Shepherd, *The Living Mountain* (Edinburgh: Canongate Books, 2019).

104 Shepherd, *The Living Mountain,* ix.

105 Shepherd, *The Living Mountain,* 8.

106 Amanda Thomson, *Belonging: Natural Histories of Place, Identity and Home* (Edinburgh: Canongate Books, 2022), 295.

107 "Common Prayer for Earth and for Humanity: Prayer for the fifth anniversary of the encyclical *Laudato Si',*" Pope Francis, *Regina Caeli,* May 24, 2020.

108"Want to Pray for Your Neighbourhood?" 24–7 Prayer website, https://www.24-7prayer.com/join_in_posts/prayer-walking.

109 Quoted in Renate Craine, *Hildegard: Prophet of the Cosmic Christ* (New York: Crossroad, 1997), 72.

110 *The Autobiography of St. Ignatius of Loyola,* section 30, in George E. Ganss, ed., Ignatius of Loyola: *The Spiritual Exercises and Selected Works* (Mahwah, NJ: Paulist Press, 1991).

111 "The Deer's Cry," http://www.irishchaplaincyparis.fr/2013/03/the-deers-cry-a-hymn-by-st-patrick.

112 Adapted from Ganss, Ignatius of Loyola [230–37]; English et al., *Twenty-four Spiritual Exercises,* 139–44; and Laurence L. Gooley, SJ, *To Walk with Christ: Praying with the Spiritual Exercises of St. Ignatius* (Saint Louis, MO: The Institute of Jesuit Sources, 2002), 115–17.

113 English et al., *Twenty-four Spiritual Exercises,* 140.

114 English et al., *Twenty-four Spiritual Exercises,* 139.

115 Adapted from Spiritual Exercises of Ignatius of Loyola, #230–37.

116 Translation by Eric Jensen, SJ, using a Latin version approved and used by Ignatius.

117 "For Movement as One," in Michelle Fraser, *Love Makes Us Beautiful: A Book of Blessings* (Self-published, 2012).

118 Sisters of Providence, *The Love of Christ Impels Us: Providence Retreat in Everyday Life* (Spokane, WA: privately published, 1991), 189.

Notes

Notes

Notes

Notes

Notes

Notes

Notes

ENVIRONMENTAL BENEFITS STATEMENT

The Publishers saved the following resources by printing the pages of this book on chlorine-free paper made with 100% post-consumer waste.

TREES	WATER	ENERGY	SOLID WASTE	GREENHOUSE GASES
16 FULLY GROWN	**1,300** GALLONS	**7** MILLION BTUs	**55** POUNDS	**6,860** POUNDS

Environmental impact estimates were made using the Environmental Paper Network Paper Calculator 4.0. For more information visit www.papercalculator.org